W9-BAF-817

IS HOLINESS REALLY POSSIBLE?

Is Holiness Really Possible?

By
David Kendall
Everett Leadingham, Editor

Though this book is designed for group study,
it is also intended for personal enjoyment and
spiritual growth. A leader's guide is available
from your local bookstore or your publisher.

Beacon Hill Press of Kansas City
Kansas City, Missouri

Copyright 2000
by Beacon Hill Press of Kansas City

ISBN: 083-411-7770

Printed in the
United States of America

Editor: Everett Leadingham
Assistant Editor: Charlie L. Yourdon
Executive Editor: Randy Cloud
Editorial Committee: Philip Baisley, Randy Cloud, Everett Leadingham,
Thomas Mayse, Larry Morris, Darlene Teague, Charlie L. Yourdon

Cover design: Michael Walsh
Cover photo: Mike Greenlar/The Image Works

Unless otherwise indicated, all Scripture references are from the *Holy Bible, New International Version*® (NIV®). Copyright © 1973, 1978, 1984 by International Bible Society. Used by permission of Zondervan Publishing House. All rights reserved.

Permission to quote from the following copyrighted versions of the Bible is acknowledged with appreciation:

The *New Revised Standard Version* (NRSV) of the Bible, copyright 1989 by the Division of Christian Education of the National Council of the Churches of Christ in the USA. All rights reserved.

The *Contemporary English Version* (CEV). Copyright © by American Bible Society 1991, 1992.

10   9   8   7   6   5   4   3   2   1

Contents

Introduction

About the Author: Dr. David Kendall is former senior pastor of the Free Methodist Church, McPherson, Kansas, and is currently superintendent of the Great Plains Conference of the Free Methodist Church. Dr. Kendall has earned a Ph.D. in biblical studies.

IT WOULD BE HARD TO READ the Bible without observing the importance of holiness. In its pages the writers constantly call God holy, and God calls His people to be holy. In fact, it is simply a given: the people of God are to be holy. They are "saints" or, as the word literally means, "holy ones."

Yet, both inside and outside the church *unholiness* abounds. Tragically, in both arenas—church and world—the *same* unholiness abounds. Let me give you an example.

I received an E-mail message from a wonderful lady in our church. The few short lines read: "I'm writing to ask for your prayers. Tom and I have serious marriage problems. I don't know what to do. My heart is breaking. Please pray." When the truth came out, I learned that Tom had gotten involved with another woman. I was floored. Of all the men I knew, *he* would have been last on the list to commit adultery. Obviously his outgoing and friendly manner, which everyone considered a special grace, masked a deep and destructive dishonesty.

This life is but one sad example of the glaring contrast between the Bible's call to holiness and the way people actually live—certainly outside the church, but also sometimes within the church. I have no trouble believing what the pollsters are telling us these days.

Recent surveys suggest that a majority of Americans have made a "personal commitment to God." Most of these would agree with traditional Christian beliefs—the Bible is the Word of God, Christ is the Savior of the world, prayer changes things, and the like. Yet, survey responses demonstrate very little practical difference in the way these "believers" live from unbelievers. When it comes to such things as basic honesty (when no one is watching), faithfulness in marriage, the use of time and money, "believing" seems to make little difference. Such surveys clearly reflect the "real life" I see in my community and church.

This "real life" haunts me because it promises no future. The brokenness I've described, which can be found everywhere, only leads to more brokenness. The "easy believism" of popular religion, even if called Christian, cannot heal the brokenness.

But God can! He himself is holy, and He calls us to be holy. His desire is for Christians to be set apart to be holy, to be separated from sin and dedicated to God. Sanctification is God's act by which He makes people holy. However, sanctification is not something that God does against human will. Sanctification is something that humans decide to seek and that God imparts.

Christians of Wesleyan heritage believe that sanctification includes the two "crises" of initial and entire sanctification. Initial sanctification takes place when a person is born again. Entire sanctification is a second work of grace that includes a lifelong process of growth, in cooperation with and enabled by the Holy Spirit.

The following chapters will take a close look at the practical aspects of not just experiencing the initial point of holiness but the ongoing implications of actually living holy lives. Holiness is a broad topic and includes a number of issues, so it is impossible for a book of this size to be a comprehensive treatment of the doctrine of sanctification. Therefore, I have concentrated on those practical aspects that will help Christians along the lifelong process of growth.

Since the book is practical rather than theoretical, its pages are filled with helpful images and examples. However, no example can be taken too far, because every human analogy eventually fails to fully represent the holiness of God. Still, good examples can move us closer to being the holy people God wants us to be.

In what follows I will share God's call to live the holy life. I have considered this call in three parts. In part one we begin with God. We will explore the foundation that God's holiness lays for human holiness. In part two we focus on the Bible's understanding of human holiness. In part three, we ask the question: "What does holiness look like in the lives of holy people?"

The common theme throughout all these pages is this: holy people are like Jesus. Let me tell you about one. Ruth approaches her 70s these days. She has been a Christian most of her life and would gladly claim the traditions of her Holiness church. She could tell you about God's sanctifying work in her life. Yet above all, Ruth follows Jesus faithfully and joyfully. She takes up her cross daily to follow. In partnership with her husband, she enjoys family life on a budget that cares for their needs but allows them to give generously for the needs of others. Ruth loves people and eagerly serves them. When the church encourages us to build bridges to unbelievers, she scours the neighborhood for the few she hasn't yet met. Soon they're over for pie and, before you know it, they're calling to ask for her prayers because they know she cares.

Ruth not only cares about the neighbor who is near but also about people all around the world. Jesus' love for the whole world has taken her on short-term missions trips and has prompted her to do without so that others with nothing might have reason to know God loves them.

Aging has now taken its toll on Ruth (though she's not the sort of person you would call "old"). Less energy, unexpected surgery, and other signs of human wear and tear have appeared. Even so, she remains sweet, positive, and confident in the One she follows.

Although Ruth earned a "black belt" in discipleship a long time ago, she's not a loner. She needs others and seeks their fellowship as companions on the way. She joins with them in a regular rhythm of joyous worship, fervent prayer, sincere searching of the Scriptures, and exciting service to others.

I don't know a more faithful follower of Jesus. And I don't know a person who better models the holiness to which God calls us all.

So to those who may have looked at the world around them and maybe have even examined their own lives and sincerely asked, "Is holiness really possible?" this book answers with a confident and challenging "Yes!"

CHAPTER 1

Is Anything Sacred Anymore?

"IT WAS THE BEST OF TIMES, it was the worst of times." With these words Charles Dickens began his classic *A Tale of Two Cities.* Certainly this sentence also describes the modern world. At the same time we see some very good things *and* some very bad things going on in our world. Where we focus determines whether we see the best or the worst.

Yet, Dickens's sentence could describe our world in a way it could not have described his own. For the modern world, the "best" and the "worst" of times depends on personal choice. One person decides what he or she sees is good, while another decides it's bad. Who's to say which one is right? No one, since every person *chooses* a perspective.

Our culture has adopted this way of thinking as a foundational principle of life. "Beauty is in the eye of the beholder," we have long said. But now so is truth and error, right and wrong, the sacred and profane. Each individual chooses. Philosophers and theologians call this "relativism."

When we base our lives on the idea that everyone must choose for himself or herself, we're building on shifting sand. If we want to see how things have changed in our culture, we only need to look at when our grandparents were young.

When our grandparents were young, abortion was not legal. Now our society supports an abortion industry that makes millions of dollars every year. Sadly, most of these abortions serve as an extreme but effective form of birth control! Only about three percent of abortions involve situations of rape, incest, or danger to the mother's life. When left to individual choice, the sacredness of human life is questionable.

When our grandparents were young, marriages lasted longer. Now, most people do not even think of divorce as odd, much less wrong. Individual choice makes the sacredness of marriage depend on personal opinion.

When our grandparents were young, sex was usually restricted to loving commitment within the bonds of matrimony. Now sex sells, entertains, and offers a form of recreation. It seems to be the center and goal of living.

When our grandparents were young, a person's word was sacred. Now research indicates that lying and cheating have become a way of life for many. These days no one will be impressed if you say, "You have my word on it!" Once you could buy most anything with such assurance. Now you couldn't rent a video!

When our grandparents were young, religion—especially Christian faith—was sacred. Now Christian faith competes with all sorts of spiritual options. In fact, Christianity is often held up for ridicule by the media and arts.

Still, you may be thinking, what does all this have to do with me or with the Christians I know? We're not relativists! Of course we're not—intentionally. Yet, we must guard against the influence of this way of thinking that our society accepts without question. Here are some questions that have made me wonder whether I'm as free from relativism as I thought. How is it possible that . . .

. . . people in my own wonderful congregations have chosen to abort a child?

. . . hardly anyone experiences shock when a professing Christian couple separates and divorces, as though the church has adopted a "no fault" divorce policy?

. . . studies show an alarming number of young people from Bible-believing churches are sexually active?

. . . Sunday ball games so easily claim the attention and devotion of people who normally come to church?

When individual choice determines what is sacred, eventually we're left wondering: Is *anything* sacred anymore? If so, on what basis can we make that claim? To answer, we must consider God's holiness.

Sacredness Matters Because God Is Holy

The Bible speaks clearly and often of holiness. Consider two striking examples. In the sixth century before Christ, God called Isaiah to serve as a prophet to His people. King Uzziah had just died, and it seemed that a sense of the loss of sacredness prevailed. Chaos ruled politically, socially, and personally for the people of God. In that time of crisis, God gave Isaiah a vision of His awesome throne in heaven. He saw frightening but beautiful creatures, serving the Lord and calling to each other in thunderous voices, "Holy, holy, holy is the LORD Almighty; the whole earth is full of his glory" (6:3).

Make no mistake, those were desperate times for the people of God. Big problems begged for solutions. God *launched* Isaiah's great work as a prophet with an affirmation of His holiness.

In the first century A.D., John discovered the same truth. He found himself a political prisoner for his faith in Jesus. The authorities banished him alone to a barren island. Yet, John had an inkling that God was about to do something big. What God showed John became our Book of Revelation.

John was "in the Spirit" one Lord's day when he had the vision. Like Isaiah, he saw a throne room in heaven. At the center, God was seated in dazzling splendor. Around God, four living creatures constantly called out, "Holy, holy, holy is the Lord God Almighty, who was, and is, and is to come" (4:8).

Again, make no mistake about it. There was much wrong in John's world. But first things first. John's understanding of how God will deal with the mess of His world *began* with a vision of the holy.

All through the Bible, God is called holy by the various writers and by God himself. Obviously in God's view, sacredness, or holiness, matters supremely. Furthermore, the experience of Isaiah and John show us a key insight. In order to make right what has gone wrong in our world, we must come to terms with the holiness of God.

What Does It Mean to Say "God Is Holy"?

The term "holy" in both the Old and New Testaments means "different, separate, unique." To say that God is holy is to say God is like no other; He is essentially different from other things or persons.

The very first pages of the Bible show us God's holiness, even though the writer does not use holiness terms. Before anything was, God was. That's why the story begins with the phrase, "In the beginning God" (Genesis 1:1). We can say that *only* of God. Then day after day during the week of creation, God said, "Let there be," and there was (see vv. 3-31). That, too, *only* applies to God. In other words, God stands above or apart from all that He created. In the story of creation, the writer always keeps the difference between God and the world clear. That's another way of saying God is holy.

When we forget or reject God's holiness, it isn't long before we confuse God with other things or persons. That's what happened in the ancient world, and it happens in our world. For example, in ancient times some people thought the physical world *was* God. Others looked to natural forces, the change of seasons, or the movement of stars and planets as God. In our world, people do much the same when they consult horoscopes, honor "Mother Earth," or seek guidance from the dead. They confuse God with what He created.

Ancient peoples also thought of the gods in human terms. Reading their mythology is like watching Saturday morning cartoons featuring various superheroes. They're bigger and stronger than ordinary people but still basically human. Understanding the gods in this way offered ancient peoples the hope of some day becoming godlike. And it still goes on today. Modern self-help programs and new-age spirituality stress the god or godlike potential within each person. Both ancient and modern worlds confuse God the Creator with what He has created.

I sometimes wonder if we're not guilty of confusing God with creation when we think about God only in friendly, "buddy-buddy" terms. Certainly God loves us. Jesus invited His disciples to think of their relationship with Him as friendship (see John 15:14-15). There's no doubt about it: God comes near and would like to establish an intimate relationship with us. But if God is only our "good buddy," we risk lowering God to the level of our human friends. That could lead to disaster. When the best of our friends tell us we should do something, we feel perfectly free to disagree. Though our friends may be disappointed for a while, we're confident they'll "come around" eventually.

God is not simply or only our Friend. God is also King, awesome and powerful. We must always understand ourselves as His servants. The truth of God's friendship with us and His kingship over us has to be kept in mind. When God tells us something, and we do otherwise, we've confused God the Creator with His creation. Also, we may be sure that God will not "come around"!

When we confuse the Creator with creation, we deny God's holiness. That's bad enough. What's more, though, we are just a couple steps away from denying that anything is holy or sacred. Think it through. If God is like creation, then everything is basically the same—which means nothing is sacred.

However, that's not what the Bible teaches. It shows us that sacredness, or holiness, does exist. Above all, the living God, Creator of all things, is holy. Because God is holy, He must hold a special (unique) place in the universe and our lives. Recapturing a sense of God's holiness provides the key to restoring the lost sense of sacredness in our lives and world.

If God's holiness means that God is unlike other things and persons, what sort of special place must God hold for us? In the remainder of this chapter, we will consider one answer and see what it means for us.

God Is Absolutely Independent

God created all things and persons. Therefore, whatever exists owes that existence to God. God the Creator is independent, and the creation is dependent.

Many people have an aquarium in their home. The water environment of an aquarium must be a carefully maintained. When we take proper care of this watery world, fish, algae, and underwater plant life thrive. All these life forms depend completely on the environment that someone else has created and maintained.

Think of it! The air we breathe, the water we drink, the food we eat, the clothing we wear, the work we do, the opportunities we have, the family and friends we enjoy—all that makes life rich, full, and satisfying comes as a gift from God. Like fish in the aquarium, we depend on God for these blessings and more. Understanding God's holiness teaches us not to take them for granted but to celebrate them as signs of our deep dependence on God.

Although most of creation cannot understand their dependence on God, human beings can know the God who made us and sustains us. The apostle Paul said, "In him [the creator God] we live and move and have our being" (Acts 17:28). How tragic when we seek to be independent from God. How foolish, in fact. Think of it! We could be like fish or algae in an aquarium that believe *they* are responsible for the watery environment that makes life possible.

God's holiness helps us understand the instructions He gives His people. We should not view God's law as rules laid down for no good reason. Rather, it expresses God's holiness and helps us understand our relationship of dependency on God. Since God is independent, He certainly has the right to show us how life works. Also, since we are dependent on God, we need the direction He gives in His Word.

Consider the Ten Commandments. Clearly they express God's holiness and lead us to live in dependence upon Him. The first four commands (which address the people's relationship with God) especially point to God as the incomparable Lord who calls us to live in a unique way. Let me illustrate with the first two commands how God's instructions serve His holiness.

The first command is, "You shall have no other gods before [or besides] me" (Exodus 20:3). As God's people, we must never regard another thing or person the way we regard God. Every once in a while we should ask whether anything has taken a godlike place in our lives—spouse, children, work, career goals, sports, or hobbies. Many things can become godlike for us, almost without our realizing it. When they do, it always spells disaster. God's command helps us avoid the disaster and enjoy a God-dependent life.

The second command is, "You shall not make for yourself an idol in the form of anything in heaven above or on the earth beneath or in the waters below" (v. 4). Most of us do not have to worry about idols in the sense of *physical* images troubling us. Yet, all of us tend to create *mental* images of God and His ways that may deeply trouble us.

On December 31, 1984, eight-year-old Amy Jo entered the hospital for routine surgery to remove a cyst on her right hand. "A simple procedure. In and out," the doctor promised. After more than an hour in the waiting room, her parents became concerned. Then several more hours threw them into a panic.

"Amy Jo just wouldn't wake up," the doctor finally reported. Later investigation revealed that one of the machines malfunctioned, mixing the gases in an incorrect and deadly way. How tragic and unfair it seemed!

For a long time, Amy's parents questioned how God could be so cruel to allow their little girl to die. We understand some of their deep pain and sorrow. Still, Amy's death created a crisis in their faith because they had embraced an image of God that was false. Their image made it seem impossible for God to be real if little girls die in surgery. Of course, keeping the second command will not lessen the pain of losing a child, but it can guard us against a crisis of faith. God's instructions help us recognize His holiness and live a God-dependent life.

When Sacred Seems a Matter of Personal Choice

We must catch a vision of the Holy One, for only when we affirm God as the Sacred One at the center of everything will we get our bearings. Then the light begins to shine. Help comes.

It sounds too simple to be true, doesn't it? Our marriages become strained. We're depressed because nothing's going right. Circumstances and people have disappointed us. Tragedy all but devastates us. We lose hope as the world goes mad. Yet, God says, "Here's the way out: recognize that I am holy." Yeah, right!

Nevertheless, that *is* what God says to us. When we acknowledge the Holy One as the center of our lives, we begin to learn two important lessons.

First, *we learn to live in humility and gratitude.* When the Holy One draws near, we will confess our unholiness and unworthiness. Isaiah saw the Lord and nearly fell apart. He pronounced woe upon himself. He realized he was not fit to be in God's presence, and, by rights, he should not have survived the experience.

Similarly, when John first saw his vision of God's holiness, he fell flat on his face, as though he were dead. In the presence of the Holy One, we realize how unlike God we are.

Nevertheless, God wonderfully reaches out to those who are humbled in His holy presence. God responded to Isaiah's woe and cleansed his unclean life and lips. God picked John up off the ground and caused him to stand. He does the same for us. Despite our unworthiness, God loves us and draws us into His holy presence. In response, we learn to live with a sense of humility and gratitude. We don't deserve the good things God does in our lives—and never will—but we are deeply grateful.

Second, *we learn to live with a spirit of surrender.* We give up our claims to independence. We offer our situations and ourselves to God. As we listen for God's direction, we learn what is good, right, and true. Then we look to God for His power to live life His way.

Background Scripture: Genesis 1:1-31; Exodus 20:3-4; Isaiah 6:1-7; John 15:14-15; Acts 17:28; Revelation 4:8

CHAPTER 2

Can We Trust Anyone Anymore?

NOT LONG AGO a *New York Times* article noted that most people would say adultery is wrong. Still, surveys suggest that it has increased over the past 20 years. In the 1970s, 25 percent of women and 50 percent of men admitted having at least one affair while married. In the 1990s, these figures have jumped to 40 percent of women and 65 percent of men.

Even if the precise figures are debatable, the trend seems alarming, doesn't it? In 1950, actress Ingrid Bergman had an affair with director Roberto Rossellini. Their adulterous relationship produced a child. Incredibly, the Congress of the United States actually denounced the actress and the director for their infidelity. As a result, Bergman fled Hollywood. Today's more tolerant attitude toward unfaithfulness signals what some conclude is "moral realism." That's another way of saying that people condone what goes on around them because they feel the need to be realistic. What a high price such realism demands! It raises the question, can we trust anyone these days?

Imagine a world where no one trusts anyone.

- One morning your radio alarm clock goes off. You hear a cheery voice announcing the news: "And this just in. During the night terrorists poisoned the town's water supply. The authorities advise that without treatment most people will soon become violently ill and die. Anyone who has had a drink during the night should proceed directly to the hospital." Panic sweeps across town. Then the panic becomes anger when it turns out to be a practical joke!

- Your doctor prescribes something to treat your symptoms, but you can't be sure it will help you. Even if you become sure, you can't trust the pharmacist to give you what the doctor ordered.
- Your baby begins to experience some sort of seizure. You panic and call 911. Nobody comes.
- The restaurant people taint the food in a way you can't taste.
- The "Una-bomber" becomes the "Omni-bomber." Not just one but everybody gets a kick out of mailing bombs. Opening the mail is a blast every day.

Can you imagine what such a world would be like? On some days, I have to wonder if we're already building that kind of world.

It's not all that bad, is it? Often I see more encouraging signs than those I've cited. One of my habits as a pastor is to visit at the nursing homes in our town. I don't suppose I ever see anything more moving and wonderful than a husband or wife faithfully caring for a partner who is unable to care for himself or herself. I think of one gentleman whose wife has Alzheimer's disease. She has come to the point where she no longer recognizes him. She doesn't know what's going on at all. When he visits, her condition often keeps her from knowing he's there and always from appreciating it. Her bodily functions have slipped from her control. She will grow worse and perhaps live on for years.

Meanwhile, he also ages. His arthritis makes it more painful and difficult to get around. Yet, every day he comes to visit her. He talks lovingly with her. He wheels her around, feeds her, and puts her to bed. Why does he do these things? More than 50 years ago this gentleman said, "For better—for worse . . . in sickness and in health . . . till death us do part." When he said those words, he had no idea what lay ahead for him and his bride. Still, he made a commitment, and he keeps it to this day. What a remarkable example of a trustworthy person! What a model of faithfulness and loyalty!

Perhaps the people in our lives have blessed us by their faithfulness—parents, husband or wife, children, friends, colleagues. As we think of them, we praise God for their remarkable faithfulness.

That's just the point—they are remarkable. Trust is rare, increasingly rare. This loving husband's commitment and care impress us because we live in a world where many husbands would do something different under similar circumstances. All around us husbands abuse or abandon their wives and children, leaving years (or maybe lifetimes) of pain to overcome. Our world prompts us to wonder, can we trust anyone? Are there some commitments we can absolutely count on?

God's Holiness Means Absolute Faithfulness

As we've seen, everywhere in the Bible God is called "holy," which literally means "different" or "unique." God is not like other things and persons. Indeed, the difference between God and all else is infinite. Only God is absolutely independent. Everything (and everyone) else depends on God.

Here's another way to express the infinite difference (the holiness) of God: *God does not change.* That doesn't mean God is old-fashioned or behind the times. Rather, it means God is consistent and reliable. In other words, God is absolutely faithful. He can be counted on, even if everyone else disappoints us.

From day one, God demonstrated His faithfulness in dealing with people. In the beginning, He made people and placed them in a world that worked well. "God saw all that he had made, and it was very good" (Genesis 1:31). The first couple enjoyed plenty of good food, companionship, and something worthy and meaningful to do in the world. God provided for all their needs.

The humans thought they could do better. So Adam and

Eve decided to reject God and His holiness by trying to be independent. Like little children, people ever since have followed their example. We try to establish our *own* lives in our
own ways.

What do we do when rejected and offended by another?
When we're told to "get lost"? When someone twists our good
intentions into something else? When someone hurts us?

The relatives of a little victim screamed into the camera,
"We want him to fry!" They insisted that, even though the
shooter was only 16, he had to pay for getting his kicks by fir-
ing into the house. His reckless shots killed a three-month-old
baby as her mother was feeding her.

We all affirm the need for justice, but this family was de-
manding more. We understand how they feel. When others
offend us, we almost automatically want to respond in kind,
even if the offense is minor. When someone cuts us off on the
highway, spreads a bad word about us, criticizes us unfairly,
steals our girlfriend or boyfriend, we want to pay them back!

God is different or holy. God made us and continues to
care for us, even when we reject Him. He wants what is good
for people and works to make it so.

Therefore, even with the sting of rejection still fresh, God
made clothing for rebellious Adam and Eve (Genesis 3:21).
He promised that the bitter results of their rebellion would
not be the final word. There would be a way out (v. 15). Later,
God called Abraham to father a people who would bring
blessing to all families of the earth (12:3). God delivered those
people from slavery in Egypt. He gave them His word of in-
struction, the Law, to guide them in the good and right way.
Then, He designed a system of sacrifice. When His people did
something wrong, this system allowed them to restore their
relationship with God.

God's faithful commitment to His people brought them
into the Promised Land. Even there, the people rejected God
and His ways. Of course, their rejection of God resulted in
judgment. They suffered defeat by their enemies. Eventually

they lost their homeland, if not their lives. The survivors had to live in a hostile, foreign land.

Yet, God did not give up on His people. He remained faithful. At the right time, God sent His own Son, Jesus, into the human family. The One who is unlike us became like us, indeed became one of us. The absolutely *independent* One became *dependent*, as we are, for a time. As a result, we can see God's holiness, especially His faithfulness, in human terms. Jesus put human clothing on divine holiness.

Still, as we would expect, people in Jesus' day remained true to form as human beings. They thought they could do better than God. Once again, they rejected God by rejecting Jesus. They crucified Him on a cross.

God allowed this. As the Holy One, God went to the limit and beyond for *our* good when Jesus died. Then He raised Jesus from the dead and now, in love, He woos us to come to Him, to be His, and to let Him work in our lives for our good.

God is not finished yet! He's made some promises about how this world will end and how people will fit into the picture. Even now He's moving us toward a time when all His promises will find fulfillment. Because God is holy—absolutely faithful—this time will certainly come. Then God's holiness will be central to all of creation—a new heaven and earth. There will be no need for the sun or other lights, no need for a temple or special place to meet with God, because He, the Holy One, will be at the center. At that time, everything will be as God wills, absolutely. Everything against His best wishes for His world will be forever gone. No tears, no death, no curse. All will be well because God is absolutely faithful (see Revelation 21—22).

Can We Trust Anyone Anymore?

Can we? Are there some commitments we can count on, no matter what? Because God is holy, the answer is yes. No matter how hurtful people have been to us. No matter how unfairly life has treated us. No matter the brokenness of our experiences. And no matter the unhealthy things we may have done to cope with it all. God's plan to make it right still stands, and God's plan includes each of us. We can be certain of this because God's holiness means He can be counted on. Consider how this works in our lives.

Suppose one day that dear woman, who is now in the nursing home with Alzheimer's disease, wakes up. For some unknown reason, her right mind returns, she looks into the eyes of her husband, and she understands. She says to herself, *For years this man has faithfully and lovingly cared for me in my weakness and illness. I didn't even know he was there, but he was. I was hardly aware of my needs and couldn't do anything about them. But he knew, and he cared!* What do you suppose would happen next? Can't you just imagine her eagerly and lovingly collapsing into her husband's embrace? Certainly, together they would experience a beautiful and deep intimacy.

Something like that happens to us when we "wake up" and truly understand who God is and what God has done for us. God is holy and independent of us. God doesn't need us. Yet, God desires us, pursues our best interests, and cares for us. He cared even when we were so out of it we didn't know what was going on. When we were in a kind of sinful stupor, clueless about our condition, God was absolutely faithful. He loved us, sent His Son to die for us, and drew us to himself.

When all this sinks in, when we wake up to these facts—if we ever truly do—we will want to collapse into His embrace. We will eagerly surrender to His loving intentions for us. Without doubt, we will want to follow His lead to be and to do what is good, right, and true. Then we will begin to experience a beautiful and deep intimacy with God.

In a world where trust is often scarce, here is God's answer: In absolute faithfulness to us, He seeks to draw us into an intimate love relationship with Him. Within that relationship, He—the absolutely faithful One—begins to make *us* faithful and trustworthy. As we collapse into His embrace, He makes us people of integrity.

Indeed, lack of integrity explains why we can hardly count on anyone these days. Public life does not match private life. Talk does not translate into walk, even when intentions are good.

Remember Peter's sad performance on Jesus' final night on earth? Jesus had set a somber mood among the disciples. He told them He would soon suffer the betrayal, denial, and desertion of His dearest friends. Peter stiffened his back courageously and protested, "I will not" (Mark 14:29). In effect he said, "All these other disciples may desert you, but I signed on for the long haul." Peter meant well, but we know what happened.

We've all wrestled with integrity, with making good on our best intentions. Most of us have vowed to live victorious Christian lives, to establish more consistent devotional habits, to serve the needs of others, to work on our marriages, to listen more carefully to our children (or parents), to witness to a neighbor—all with the best of intentions. Still, we've failed at some point or even entirely. When we're honest, we know how impossible these things are without help from God.

When the absolutely faithful One draws us into His embrace, He becomes the center and focus of our living. His faithfulness draws our public and private lives together and makes them one in Him. Then our intentions get translated into action. Others depend on our word. The conflict ends between what we should be and actually are and what we should do and actually do.

Some would laugh at the thought that our world needs "holiness." The very word "holy" raises strange and unattractive images in people's minds, images that hardly seem relevant for a modern world.

Yet when we listen to what God tells us in His Word, the relevance of holiness becomes clear. When we lose a sense of the sacred, we are just a step away from losing everything. The world becomes a place where the reliable and the trustworthy disappear.

The good news is that God reveals himself as the Holy One. He invites us to realize our dependence on Him and to receive the blessings He offers that we can count on. When He is at the center, He restores a sense of the sacred to us. He becomes the solid basis for rebuilding a sense of trust so necessary for meaningful relationships.

Background Scripture: Genesis 1:31; 3:15, 21; 12:3; Mark 14:29; Revelation 21—22

CHAPTER 3

Wanting to Be Holy

ALL THROUGH THE BIBLE, God calls His people to be holy. Of course, that suggests it is really possible to live a holy life. But why would we want to be holy? Most people, not all of them outside the church, do *not* have "holiness" on their list of top 10 priorities. I think I understand why.

The very word "holy" often brings bizarre things to people's minds. For some, "holy" means "holier than thou." In some parts of our country, people expect the "holy" to handle snakes and drink poison as proof of their faith. In other places, the word "holy" transmits images of the sour, stiff, stuffy, stingy, and somber. A "holy" person would be standoffish, inhibited, prudish, fearful, and joyless. If "holiness" means any of this, who needs it? Who wants it?

Being holy, however, has nothing to do with such things. When the Bible says we may be holy, it's announcing good news. Consider three quick reasons why.

First, suppose we could be all we were meant to be. Wouldn't that be good? When we are holy, as the Bible understands holy, we are the way God meant us to be.

Second, suppose we could be like Jesus. Wouldn't that be good? Is there a more attractive and inviting person in history? The great Mahatma Gandhi of India once said, "I am not a Christian because I've never met anyone like Jesus. If I did, maybe I'd become one." How good it would be for the world to be full of people like Jesus. That would be a world full of "holy" people.

Third, suppose the world were full of people just as they were meant to be and just like Jesus. Wouldn't that help to solve most of the problems we see around us or face in our lives?

Our world desperately needs holiness, rightly understood and powerfully real in human life. In truth, there could hardly be better news than this: according to the Bible, we may be holy.

Yet, we must carefully observe our use of "holy." As we've seen in the Bible, God is the Holy One. That means God is incomparable, with no equal, in a class all alone. Obviously, then, we are not and never could be holy as God is holy. No matter how saintly we may be, there will always be an infinite difference between God and us.

Still, the Bible applies this word "holy" to people. How can people—ordinary human beings so totally beneath God, people like us—be called "holy"? Let's see how the Bible answers that question.

The Big Problem

Almost from the beginning, the human race decided to reject God's holiness. The first temptation challenged God's holy character. "God knows that when you eat of [the forbidden fruit] your eyes will be opened, and *you will be like God*" (Genesis 3:5, emphasis added). The serpent suggested there was no real difference between God and us that a little fruit wouldn't cure. When Adam and Eve gave in to the temptation, they tried to be more like God than God made them to be and rejected God's holiness. They were rebelling against God's rule as Lord of creation, thinking they could improve on God's world.

Their rejection of God hardly brought improvements. Instead, rebellion against God became a way of life for their children. This rebellion, in turn, has brought ruin to everything and everyone. In the Book of Genesis, once they rejected God's holiness, nothing worked right. The whole world of nature—plants and animals—changed forever. Humans suffered distortion in mind, body, spirit, and emotions. No relationship in life escaped.

Like ripples in a pond, the first couple's "no" to God's ho-

liness shapes every person's life. The apostle Paul explained
this to Christians in Rome using the family as an illustration.
Adam, head of the human household, made a bad choice.
That choice has brought pain and suffering to the whole family. We never live down the powerful impact of Adam's mis-
deeds. Instead, all of Adam's children, including us, tend to do
what Adam did (see Romans 5:12-21). Just as small children
eventually walk, talk, and make gestures like their parents—
developing the same habits and adopting the same attitudes
—so we end up like our first parents.

Unfortunately, some of us have had better opportunity
than others to understand the pain of this common human reality. Our parents abused us. Perhaps they became addicted to
some substance. Or maybe they suffered a severe emotional
disorder. Often we discover that their parents suffered in the
same ways. Now we battle it too. The cycles of misery and defeat passed from generation to generation in some of our families give us a painful parable of what has happened to the
whole human family.

When we come into this world, therefore, we are pro-
grammed for rebellion against God. We will seek any way but
God's way. What seems normal to us has little in common
with what God planned for us. In our "natural" ways, we don't
recognize God as Creator and King. We try to live a God-free
life, but where does that lead us? Since God determines the
good, right, and true, we lose our moral and spiritual bearings. We are convinced that we can define those standards for
ourselves. We become intensely centered on self. We value
people and things as they serve our own self-interest. We are
loving, kind, generous, and helpful—when it advances our
cause.

When you peel back the layers covering modern life, isn't
that what's going wrong in marriages, families, and communities? Self-centeredness has ruined our relationships. When the
Bible speaks of human nature as "sinful" (Romans 7:18), it

refers to this programming we've received from Adam and its consequences.

We are not holy because we are sinful and deeply damaged by our rebellion against God. The damage touches every part of us, and that's a big, big problem.

The Amazing Fact

Despite this big problem, the Bible still insists we may be holy. Clearly, God finds ways to share His holiness. On a regular basis, people, places, and things are called "holy" in the Bible. In both the Old and New Testaments, God describes His people as holy, and God judges them when they are not holy. Hebrews even says, "Without holiness no one will see the Lord" (Hebrews 12:14). Obviously, people (along with places and objects) may share in the holiness of God. How?

Quite simply, *God's presence makes people, places, and things holy.* When God comes near, persons and things do not remain the same.

Moses was wandering around in the desert near Mount Horeb, tending his sheep when, unexpectedly, he saw wisps of smoke in the air. As he came near, he could see a bush on fire, but it wasn't burning up. He approached it until God shouted, "Do not come any closer . . . Take off your sandals, for the place where you are standing is holy ground" (Exodus 3:5). That patch of wilderness soil became holy because God was there. In time, Moses himself became a totally different person for the same reason—God was with him. God's presence makes places and people holy.

Probably you have had personal experiences that brought this truth home, even if you didn't relate it to holiness. In a worship service, for example, when God made His presence known—perhaps through a special ministry of music, in moments of silent prayer, or when the truth of the Word grips your heart—you've sensed God making the sanctuary and that moment different or holy. Or when you first committed your life to Christ, you knew God had come to live within you, and you were different. As you were experiencing the close presence of God, He was sharing His holiness with you! Simply put, if we live close to God, we live a holy life.*

When we live a holy life, we may expect two consequences. First, *we are able to see our human condition clearly.* In God's presence, we see ourselves for who, and how, we are. Isaiah the prophet experienced this in the Temple. He cried out as God came near, "Woe is me! I'm ruined, doomed. I am unclean in lips and life, and so are my people" (Isaiah 6:5, author's paraphrase). In the light of God's presence, we see where our lives clash with God's character.

Peter had the same experience one day when Jesus gave him a miraculous catch after a disappointing night of fishing. Instead of celebrating his success, he collapsed in a heap at Jesus' feet and said, "Go away from me, Lord; I am a sinful man!" (Luke 5:8). Peter suddenly realized that Jesus was God, and in the presence of the holy God, he could see his own unholiness.

Indeed, in God's holy presence, we easily recognize thoughts, attitudes, actions, and reactions that do not match God's. Of course, we must then make a choice between God's way and ours.

A few years ago, I went to a conference with hopes of being encouraged and renewed in my pastoral ministry. When the conference began, I would have explained my need by telling you about some folk in the church who seemed picky and easily distracted from truly important things. Their attitudes blocked what God wanted to do in the church. So I prayed, "Lord, touch me, fill me, but whatever You do, by all means straighten *them* out!"

The Lord did touch me in a wonderful way. During the opening service, God's Spirit invaded the sanctuary of my heart, and I knew I was in the awesome presence of the Lord. All of a sudden I saw my heart and my attitude as God saw them.

To my utter surprise, the Lord gently but powerfully showed me that I had been even more distracted than anyone in the church. In my mind, the Lord replayed several recent encounters with my daughter and reminded me of the irritation I had because her youth activities had inconvenienced me. No, it was more than irritation—it was anger. In a burst of painful insight, I realized that my irritation-turned-to-anger over driving her around town kept her from sharing the best news of her life—her recent commitment to the Lord! Even worse, I had put myself in a position where I couldn't help her take important spiritual steps. I—who had prayed for the Lord to work this way in her life and had mentally cast stones at others in the church—was in the wrong. I saw so clearly that I was the one who needed to be changed by God. When we are in His holy presence, God helps us to see our condition so that He may draw us closer and make us like Him.

Second, when we begin to live in God's presence and share His holiness, *we are called to serve.* In God's holy presence, one of the things we see so clearly is that God keeps busy. God works in all sorts of ways for the good of people. Therefore, as we live in His presence, we are not only drawn to *be* like God is but also to *do* what God does in the world.

That was the experience of Moses. Encountering God in His holiness gave him something to do, even though he didn't feel at all qualified. That was also the experience of Isaiah. Before long, he heard himself saying, "Lord, I'm here, send me. Use me. I'll serve!" (Isaiah 6:8, author's paraphrase). Peter's response matches the others. When he fell before Jesus, Jesus reassured him that he would soon be fishing for people (Luke 5:10).

That's also the way it worked with me. In the opening session of that conference, once God's holy presence revealed where I did not match God, I was moved to repent and to trust God to change me. Then I quickly realized there were some things I had to do because of the deepened sense of God's holy presence in my life. Throughout the rest of the two-day conference, the Lord showed me what to do. To begin, I had to repair the damaged relationship with my daughter, celebrate her commitment to the Lord, and pledge to support all God was doing in her life. Then I had to make a full confession to my church family and lead them in seeking first God's kingdom and His righteousness.

The next Sunday morning, as I shared these things with my church family, God's Holy Spirit moved among our people. God, in His holiness, visited us and many moved into a deeper relationship with the Lord. I was the first one to the altar.

When God is present in our lives, we are holy. As we share in His holiness, we see where we do not match His character and are drawn to be like Him. Likewise, we are drawn to do what God does in the world around us.

The Wonderful Gift

What about that big problem? How could we really be like God and do as God does when we are sinful? What can be done about the unholiness that seems so natural to us?

Jesus is the gift of holiness. The God who is totally unlike us became like us in Jesus. We can see what holiness looks like and how holiness behaves by watching Jesus. That's how we know those unattractive and bizarre views of holiness are wrong. Jesus was not like that.

We begin to be holy people by joining ourselves to Jesus, by following Christ. Our initial steps in following Him become the first steps in a holy life. That's what happened to Peter and the others who first followed Jesus. He called them and, in following Him, they became different, or holy, people. As they walked with Jesus, they began to live in a different way. They did and said things as never before. They went places they'd never visited before and related to people and circumstances in new ways. What made them different? Being with Jesus, the Holy One. When He was with them, and they with Him, they were holy.

Of course, they were not perfect. They still needed God to work powerfully in their lives. God had to deal with their rebellion and to heal the wounds of their past lives. Becoming new or holy people—increasingly like Jesus in character and lifestyle—began when they determined to join Jesus' movement. That's how it begins with us too. That's why most people feel as though things are different when they commit their lives to Jesus for the very first time. Things *are* different. They are walking through life with Jesus, which means never being the same again. His death and resurrection open up a new way to be and to live. In Jesus, God gives us a new family where the same old cycle of rejecting God's way is broken. In our new family, we find freedom from rebellion and self-centeredness, freedom to live in godlike ways as Jesus did.

Who Wants to Be Holy?

No right-thinking person wants to handle snakes, drink poison, or withdraw into weirdness and oddity. Nobody wants to become stiff, sour, or sad. And nobody really wants to be "holier-than-thou." God doesn't want these things either.

Most people want to be the way we were meant to be. Most feel the attraction of a Christlike life. Almost everyone would agree that to be like Jesus—to be as we were meant to be—would be good, not only for us but for our world. In fact, that's exactly what God wants.

Background Scripture: Genesis 3:5; Exodus 3:5; Isaiah 6:5, 8; Luke 5:8, 10; Romans 5:12-21; 7:18; Hebrews 12:14

---

*Though we establish a beginning of holy life when we are justified, at the point of sanctification we move decidedly further into holiness.

CHAPTER 4

Forgiveness

WE HAVE SEEN that God calls us to be holy. Even more, God assures us we may be holy. Not weird, not "holier-than-thou," but like Jesus. Jesus is God's presence with us and within us. God's presence in our lives makes us holy. How does it happen? How does God move us from being like we are (naturally) to being like Jesus (supernaturally)?

Let me tell you about John and Candace. During their college years, John fell in love with Candace and pursued her affections. The pursuit came easy for John, who was outgoing, fun loving, and good-looking. John was "the life of the party." For Candace, however, John's pursuit made life uncomfortable, because she was shy, reserved, and thought of herself as rather plain. Candace was the wallflower at the party. Certainly Candace did not have a problem with pride. To the contrary, she couldn't believe anyone, especially someone like John, would be interested in her.

So John had his work cut out for him. He would have to be very creative to get her attention and convince her of his love. John was up to the task. He showered her with flowers regularly. Once, Candace returned to her room to find it filled with balloons. Then John commissioned Candace's friends as special messengers to tell her of his love. Finally, before he had to rent the skywriting plane, she got the message. A year later, John and Candace married.

However, the story does not end with a simple "happily ever after," though at first it seemed that way. In the years that followed, John and Candace had two daughters, moved to a major metropolitan area, and began a successful small business. Life treated the family well. The girls made their parents proud, and Candace had begun to come out of her shell. She believed in her God-given abilities and felt a deepening life partnership with John.

Then one evening, everything fell apart with a phone call. Candace answered, and the woman's voice asked for John. Somehow it didn't feel right, and the more Candace thought about it the more other questions came to mind. Questions about what she had seen and sensed in recent months. It took several days for the story to surface fully. John had enrolled in a graduate program. In one of his classes he'd met a young woman. One thing led to another, until an out-of-town "business trip" became a cover for a rendezvous between lovers. John's unfaithfulness devastated Candace, their girls, their home, and their faith.

Eight hundred years before Jesus' birth, God told His people that's how He felt. God was an absolutely faithful partner, but something went wrong with the marriage. His people left Him for other lovers. So God called the prophet Hosea to model the pain God felt and the response God would make. What a tough assignment! "When the LORD began to speak through Hosea, the LORD said to him, 'Go, take to yourself an adulterous wife and children of unfaithfulness, because the land is guilty of the vilest adultery in departing from the LORD.' So he married Gomer daughter of Diblaim, and she conceived and bore him a son" (1:2-3).

As expected, Gomer proved unfaithful. She abandoned Hosea for other lovers, and eventually, her unfaithfulness brought deep pain to herself as well as her husband. Perhaps you know from personal experience the devastation of a marriage shattered by adultery. You understand the pain of Candace, Hosea, and God.

Indeed, God tells us that's the way it is between Him and us, His people. In our natural state, we are painfully separated from God and at odds with God. Even though God made us for himself so that our well-being depends on a loving and holy relationship with Him, we have broken that relationship.

The pain and brokenness of Candace and Hosea offer a parable of our unfaithfulness toward God. Can a relationship so badly damaged be repaired? Can that relationship be special, holy, ever again? If so, how?

God Takes Action for Us

God refuses to settle for pain and brokenness. Instead, He pursues us. He seeks us where we are, arranging or rearranging our circumstances, working through them, around them, or sometimes against them to get our attention and draw us to himself. God announced His intentions through Hosea: "Therefore I am now going to allure her; I will lead her into the desert and speak tenderly to her" (2:14). Then He spoke directly to His unfaithful people:

"'In that day,' declares the LORD, 'you will call me "my husband"; you will no longer call me "my master." . . . I will betroth you to me forever; I will betroth you in righteousness and justice, in love and compassion. I will betroth you in faithfulness, and you will acknowledge the LORD'" (2:16, 19-20).

In other words, God responds to our unfaithfulness by taking action that will bring us into a special, holy relationship with Him despite our unfaithfulness. Ultimately, this divine response to human sin led Jesus to die on the Cross. The First Epistle of John says, "This is love: not that we loved God, but that he loved us and sent his Son as an atoning sacrifice for our sins" (4:10). To be sure, if we love God, it is only because God first loved us (see v. 19).

God's response to the brokenness of our relationship with Him makes possible a new relationship of love. God always makes the first move, seeking to woo us and win us to a relationship of love and intimacy. Perhaps we're tempted to think that because God is great and mighty, what He has done is easy, no big deal. Yet, consider three huge barriers standing between God and us.

For one, *the barrier of a broken heart*. Imagine the pain Candace felt when John betrayed her. Recall the rejection you have felt in the past, the heartbrokenness. "Heartache" seems an understatement when describing the soul-deep anguish of such betrayal. Now imagine God, infinite in ability because He is God. That means infinite in His ability to feel pain and rejection. Surely the most devastating human broken-hearted-ness barely begins to approach God's. Yet God pursues us!

There is also *the barrier of unjust rejection.* It's painful to be rejected under any circumstances, but the sting reaches deep-er when the rejection comes in response to love. John could claim no innocence or excuse for his unfaithfulness. Likewise, Gomer's abandonment of Hosea had no legitimate basis. In both cases, it's just plain wrong. Their partners had been mod-els of loyalty toward them.

Similarly, we have been in the wrong when we have re-jected or ignored the God who made us. We repaid a thou-sand or million undeserved kindnesses with blatant rebellion. Imagine it, even in our rebellion, God continued to give us good things, even the ultimately good thing: "While we were still sinners, Christ died for us" (Romans 5:8). Despite our un-just rejection of God, He pursues us!

The third barrier is that of *insensitivity.* Probably Gomer could justify her unfaithfulness. If you could ask her, she would cite some factors that, to her mind, make wrong appear right. John did the same with Candace. "If only she had been this way or that, then I wouldn't have been attracted to the other woman." How often we say or think something like this of God. "If only this hadn't happened. If only God had not al-lowed it. If I could just get a break, then maybe I would take God more seriously."

It's amazing how often the guilty will try to make those they've offended responsible for their offense. Of course, such insensitivity and self-justification only makes the barrier high-er between those who are separated. It also deepens the pain. Sadly, we have all played that game with others and with God. Still, God pursues us. What good news!

God refuses to give up on people. He sent Hosea to reclaim his unfaithful wife as an illustration of this very fact. "Go, show your love to your wife again, though she is loved by another and is an adulteress. Love her as the LORD loves the Israelites though they turn to other gods" (3:1). It's simply in the nature of God to do this, to come to where we are, to be there for us, and to draw us to himself.

Ultimately, all these loving intentions of God came to expression in Jesus. John put it like this in his Gospel: "The Word [meaning Jesus] became flesh" (1:14). God identified with us, stooped to our level in order to relate to us, as we do with our little children. Luke makes a major point of this in his Gospel by noting that Jesus was called "a friend of tax collectors and 'sinners'" (7:34)—people with the most sinful reputations. Not friendly toward sin but toward *people* whose sin broke God's heart and separated them from Him. Jesus openly welcomed them. In fact, He came "to seek and to save" them (19:10). At all costs, Jesus sought to close the gap between sinful people and a holy God. The apostle Paul declared, "God was reconciling the world to himself in Christ" (2 Corinthians 5:19), that is, powerfully at work making peace between God and us.

What about those enormous barriers—the broken heart of God, His rightful outrage over our unjust rejection of His kindness, and our rationalizations before Him? We could never deal with these barriers we've built. It requires divine demolition, which God has done for us. Jesus died to destroy the barriers. "Remember that . . . you were separate from Christ, excluded . . . , without hope and without God in the world. But now in Christ Jesus you who once were far away have been brought near through the blood of Christ" (Ephesians 2:12-13). So far as God is concerned, the way to Him is now clear and open. He calls to us, wooing us into a special, holy relationship with Him.

We Must Welcome a Loving Relationship with Him

If God "proposes," we are called to accept. In order to do this, however, we must first acknowledge the barriers. To be sure, God has dealt with them through Jesus, destroying them on the Cross, clearing the way for us to know and love Him. Still, we must acknowledge what God has done.

The barriers are real. Each of us must recognize and accept responsibility. Recognizing the barriers and the pain they've caused is called "confession" in the Bible. If we truly acknowledge the barriers, we will renounce them and turn away from all that breaks the heart of God. This "turning away" is called "repentance" in the Bible. Then the One who has sought us out and taken action for us enfolds us in His forgiveness. A new, special, holy relationship begins. Indeed, the holy life begins.

What an amazing and powerful gift is God's forgiveness! Sometimes we seriously underrate it. Perhaps we place such a high premium on "the deep things of God" (1 Corinthians 2:10) that we treat forgiveness as a small gift, merely preliminary to the "real" gift, which is holiness.

It's easy to be confused by common, cultural misconceptions of what forgiveness means. One common error holds that forgiveness means *indifference*. God pats us on the head, "There, there, that's OK!" Another misconception would suggest forgiveness means *denial*. "You didn't mean it; no harm done." A third mistake is to make forgiveness a form of *indulgence*. "Love is never having to say you're sorry."

In truth, however, receiving forgiveness from God requires that "we get real." Our offense against God wasn't OK. It was tragically, fatally wrong. It brought great hurt to God, to others, and to us. We *did* mean it, and the outcome required supreme sacrifice—the death of Jesus. What a large and wonderful gift is God's forgiveness! In fact, forgiveness is nothing less than a miracle.

The miracle moves both ways between God and us. Obviously, as we've seen, God's deep love flows toward us as He removes the painful barriers separating us from Him. When God forgives us, He also gives us the capacity to love Him, deeply and passionately, with all that we are. This new love for God signals the holy life.

Great Forgiveness Leads to Great Love

Once a Pharisee invited Jesus to a dinner party. As He often did, Jesus accepted the invitation and joined a number of other guests at the Pharisee's table. We imagine a cordial dinner with stimulating conversation to the delight of all. Then everything changed; a woman came to the place where Jesus reclined. For any woman to do this would have been shameful and disruptive, but *this* woman was known all over town as especially sinful. She came, weeping convulsively and carrying a jar of perfume. She bathed Jesus' feet with her tears, dried them with her hair, kissed them with her lips, and anointed them with her perfume. Everyone watched in stunned silence. No doubt some of the other guests thought the woman was having an emotional breakdown. The Pharisee, however, concluded Jesus was neither prophet nor holy. A prophet would know what sort of woman she was, and a holy man would not let her touch him.

The host and guests were wrong, as Jesus explained through a parable. This woman, like the debtor who had been forgiven an enormous debt, could not help herself. She simply had to respond with a lavish display of love. Her great love demonstrated great forgiveness. Likewise, the Pharisee, who had no awareness of the gift of forgiveness, loved little or not at all (see Luke 7:36-50).

When God forgives us, He draws us near to Him, and we begin to know this One who loves us supremely. That new relationship gives us the confidence that all is well between God and us. We are freed from fear or dread to be in God's holy presence, and we begin to love God, who first loved us. Our love relationship with God makes us different, or holy.

That's the way it worked with John and Candace, eventually. John's unfaithfulness brought the deepest pain to her and built up the highest barriers between them. Humanly speaking, there was no hope. However, Candace was no longer a wallflower. She had become a woman made strong by God's forgiving love. Despite John's devastating rejection, God made her secure in His love and in His promise to care for her. Candace dared to trust that forgiveness could become the basis for a whole new kind of relationship. Not all at once, but no less surely over time, she remained open to John and loved him again.

Don't misunderstand. Candace didn't indulge or tolerate John's unfaithfulness. Hers was a tough love that suffered the pain of betrayal and then dared to reach out again. Then, for his part, John had to face the truth about himself and his conduct. He had to feel Candace's pain and that of his children. Patiently and painstakingly, he had to rebuild the trust and reestablish their confidence in his love. Eventually it happened, and, amazingly, they now enjoy a deeper and more joyful relationship than before.

Candace opened the way for this to happen through the gift of forgiveness. John's acceptance of her gift began an entirely different, or holy, relationship.

Background Scripture: Hosea 1:2-3; 2:14, 16, 19-20; 3:1; Luke 7:34, 36-50; 19:10; John 1:14; Romans 5:8; 1 Corinthians 2:10; 2 Corinthians 5:19; Ephesians 2:12-13; 1 John 4:10, 19

CHAPTER 5

Being One with God

AFTER THE HONEYMOON, there is life. Once the excitement of the wedding and reception fades and we return from the honeymoon, we begin to make a life together as husband and wife. All the wonderful potential of marriage—"life's happiest and holiest relationship," the ceremony says—lies ahead. We want to make the most of it, experiencing all that it means to be "one."

In the same way, once God has forgiven us and we begin to enjoy a new relationship with Him, we soon discover that we have a lot to learn about God, ourselves, and our relationship with God. We have a long way to go before we experience deep oneness with God.

My wife and I were engaged a year and 10 months before we married. Let me share our story.

I arrived on the campus of a small Christian college something of a love-starved puppy. High school had disappointed me socially, mostly for lack of opportunity. When I became a serious believer, I determined I would date and marry a girl who shared my commitment to follow Jesus. Unfortunately, my small church didn't have many girls. I dated all three of them—twice.

Then a new pastor came to our church with a family full of girls. *Surely it is a godsend,* I thought. In the four years they served our church, I went through the whole family, but it led nowhere.

After graduation, I hit that small, Christian-college campus in a tragically deprived condition, which severely impaired my common sense. I felt obligated to date every girl who seemed serious about following Jesus. Three months of

tiresome effort left me worn out, brokenhearted, and disillu-
sioned. I even began to wonder if God had called me to the
single life.

Then I met Lavone. Quickly we knew we were meant for
each other. We shared common interests and values. Our con-
versations lasted long into the night and covered the most important subjects. We felt that special "chemistry" between us.

You can't believe how hard it was to wait 22 months to
get married. August 16, 1975, finally arrived, and we said, "I
do."

Now when I work with couples preparing for marriage, I
always tell them, "You really don't know what you're getting
into." I speak honestly from our experience. Lavone and I had
a wonderful courtship, engagement (except its length), and
wedding. We knew God meant us to be together, and we gave
ourselves to each other in love.

Yet it didn't take long for us to discover how little we
knew about living as "one." Here's a brief rundown on the lessons I learned about myself:

- I discovered things about myself I hadn't shared with
  Lavone because even I didn't know about them. I
  learned how much I like to do things my way. That
  made me hard to live with.
- Without even trying, I offended her. Regularly, I carried
  over practices from my former days of singleness. Often
  her tears told me how much this hurt.
- I didn't communicate very well. Talking was no problem, but really making connection with her was. My
  ears worked unreliably and sometimes not at all.

At first, these discoveries sent me into shock. We had "a
marriage made in heaven," or so I thought. We were in love,
but we could be miserable to each other. The road to oneness
seemed long indeed. We now know that's the way it works in
any relationship, including our relationship with God.

We Begin with a Love Relationship

The Bible uses the imagery of courtship and marriage to describe how God relates to us and makes us holy. As we have seen, God presents himself as a faithful suitor who woos us and wins us as His bride. Truly, *that* is the marriage made in heaven.

Of course, we shouldn't press this imagery too far. God desires and pursues us but not because He needs us. God is not love-starved or needy as I was. Rather we need God and were made for God. Likewise God does not pursue us because He finds us attractive and inviting as we are naturally. No, we have not treated God very well at all. At the least, we have ignored Him, pretending He doesn't exist or doesn't matter. In different ways, we have all rebelled against God and tried to live independently, our own way. As a result, we have offended God.

To be sure, this imagery is not perfect. But realizing its imperfections only increases our wonder that God chooses to relate to us as a groom to a bride. Unlike any romance we've ever known, God desires and pursues us simply because He loves us and wants what is best for us.

When we begin to understand what God has done in Christ Jesus and that He could really love us that much, we say, "I do." We commit ourselves to Him. Just as God claims us, we claim God. The past, with all the barriers that had kept us from God, has been swept away. Our forgiveness from God begins a relationship that promises oneness with God.

On the way to oneness we discover a lot about ourselves we never knew before. We learn that some of the ways we think, feel, and act grieve God. Communication with God challenges us. We like to talk to God but have a hard time listening so that we are in tune with Him. As we grow in our relationship with Him, all these discoveries present us with a choice.

Deepening Our Love Relationship

When we understand more fully what it means to belong to God, we have a choice to make. Will we continue to pursue this love relationship with God? Since it is a *relationship,* we must choose to continue it. Since it is a *love* relationship, God will not coerce us or force himself on us—not at the beginning or later. He draws us to oneness.

Therefore, when we learn that something in our lives does not please Him, we must deal with it. That's a choice only we can make. Yet, we don't make the choice on our own. God lovingly leads us and empowers us to deepen the relationship He has established with us. By following His lead, we will enter into oneness with Him. Throughout the Bible, we find various expressions of this basic choice to make the most of our relationship with God and pursue oneness with Him. Let me share three of them.

Whom Will You Serve?

As the Lord miraculously led the Israelites from slavery in Egypt, they began a new chapter in their relationship to God. When the Lord gave Moses the Ten Commandments, they began to understand more fully what their new life would mean. They made a unanimous decision to serve God. "We will do everything the LORD has said" (Exodus 19:8), they promised, though time would prove they had difficulty living up to their role as the people of God.

God's way of leading the children of Israel offers a model for understanding our pursuit of oneness with God through Jesus. Sooner or later we discover a basic clash of wills—ours against God's. Perhaps God wants us to make a career move or make a lifestyle adjustment that will allow us to serve Him in some way. Or maybe we struggle with His call to be in the Word, to spend more time in prayer, or to make time to meet the needs of someone near us. Sooner or later, oneness with God means we will have to say what Jesus said, "Not as I will, but as you will" (Matthew 26:39). Then the clash of wills ends, and a deeper harmony comes to our love relationship with the Lord.

Whom Will You Love?

Jesus never lost sight of the main point: we are called into an exclusive love relationship with God. "Love the Lord your God with all your heart and with all your soul and with all your mind and with all your strength" (Mark 12:30). As in any truly loving relationship, our primary concern will be clarifying and expanding our love for God. Obedience—the specific things we do or don't do—should always grow out of love for God. Indeed, our obedience and our service to God are ways of saying, "I love you."

For example, God commands us to pray, worship, and witness. Our obedience to God demands that we do these things. In our praying, we're consulting our Beloved and whispering our love to Him. In our worship, we're setting aside time out of a busy schedule to focus exclusively on Him because our relationship with Him is worth it. In our witness, we're sharing with others the love of our lives.

On the way to oneness with God, we will choose to serve God above all. Yet our service must never become anything other than love in action. Jesus leads us not to focus on rules but on love. In the absence of passionate love for God, the most perfect conformity to all the rules will count for nothing. If we choose to love God fully and passionately, we will want to please God, as all passionate lovers do their beloved. Keeping appropriate rules of conduct will never be an issue.

Whose Will You Be?

In writing to Christians in Rome, Paul urged, "Offer your bodies as living sacrifices, holy and pleasing to God—this is your spiritual act of worship. Do not conform any longer to the pattern of this world, but be transformed by the renewing of your mind" (Romans 12:1-2). The image of sacrifice leads us to think about altars. That may seem strange to our modern experience. We picture stone altars—perhaps elaborate ones we've seen in books or videos—and bloody sacrifices. What could be farther from our contemporary culture?

Yet, we are only fooling ourselves by exaggerating the differences between our time and Paul's. We also have altars, and we make sacrifices. They look different than the first-century models, but they're no less real. Television, sports arenas, computers, homes, vacation spots, and workplaces all qualify as modern altars. They represent places or pursuits to which we sacrifice, devote, or offer ourselves. Some people lay their very lives on such altars. They do it to find meaning and fulfillment in life, just as their ancient counterparts hoped to find through animal sacrifices. So with a little adjustment for our modern setting, Paul's sacrifice image can still speak powerfully to us.

In mercy, God did not reject us when we rejected Him. Instead, He sent Jesus to show us His love. Through His sacrifice, we have received a new life in right relationship with Him. God set us free from the power of sin and gave us His Spirit to empower a life pleasing to Him.

If we compare our relationship with God to a marriage, truly it is "a marriage made in heaven." Therefore, we will make sure we are entirely His. There will be no holding back; we will give our whole selves to God. That's the sacrifice we will want to make. A living sacrifice that puts all we are and have at His disposal—all our abilities, potential, strengths, and weaknesses. In a love relationship, no halfway measures or halfhearted commitments make sense. Only our utter abandonment of all to God will do.

In fact, that's the only way the relationship can work. Can you imagine a marriage where one partner says to another, "I'll give you one day out of the week"? How absurd! How about a marriage where one partner says, "I'm going to give you every day *but* one. On that day I'm on my own." Not even that would do. Partners who love one another hold nothing back. They give it all.

Oneness with God

Once God claims us as His own and forgives us, we begin a wonderful love relationship. Yet when the glory and glow of "the honeymoon" fade, there's a life to live. We will want to realize the full potential of the relationship. Only complete oneness and full intimacy with God will prove satisfying.

Intimacy requires continuing and deepening our relationship with God. God leads, we follow, and along the way we learn what our love for God means.

On August 16, 1975, I couldn't have loved my wife Lavone more. Undoubtedly, we were as committed to each other as we knew how to be at the time. We didn't want a mere "Kodak moment" for the scrapbook to show our friends the lovely wedding we had. We wanted oneness. We insisted on nothing less than all our love could promise.

So when I learned how I was and what I needed to do for our relationship to be all it could be, I began to do it. I truly loved this woman and desired a full return on her love for me. Along the way, our relationship changed, deepened. Our surrender to each other now seems full and complete in a way much different than 25 years ago. It's not a perfect marriage, and we haven't ironed out all the communication issues to our complete satisfaction. To be sure, I'm not beyond the possibility of hurting her. Still, we have a depth of relationship, a quality of yieldedness, and a level of knowing each other that convinces us we are one.

Our love relationship with God through Jesus travels a similar path. When God forgives us, we begin a special and holy relationship with Him. Just as He gave His all for us, so we give our all in return. What a wonderful love begins between us! Yet, as in any relationship, the potential for complete oneness and harmony must be worked out. And we work it out by choosing God, His will, His love, and His way above all. When we do, God brings us into deep oneness with Him. Then, with Paul, we say, "For to me, to live is Christ" (Philippians 1:21).

Background Scripture: Exodus 19:8; Matthew 26:39; Mark 12:30; Romans 12:1-2; Philippians 1:21

CHAPTER 6

Embracing the Cross

WHEN WE BEGIN TO FOLLOW JESUS, we begin to walk in a different, or holy, way. We begin a journey toward Christlikeness. For, as we've seen, to be holy is to be like Jesus.

We may wish to protest even the thought of being like Jesus. We know ourselves too well—how we think, speak, act, and react. We know what happens when the kids try our patience, the pressure mounts at work, or a hundred other common situations arise. These real-life experiences suggest that Jesus could be no more than a lofty model, perched on some impossibly high pedestal, to be admired and modestly imitated. We could never *really* be like Him —could we?

Yes! At least that's what the New Testament teaches. Wasn't that exactly what Jesus intended when He first called people to follow Him? In the Gospels, once the first disciples respond to Jesus' call, it isn't long before they're doing the very things Jesus did. In fact, He sent them out to preach the very same message He preached (the message of repentance and the coming kingdom of God). He also empowered them for the same ministries of healing and casting out demons (see Matthew 10:1; Mark 6:6-13; Luke 9:1-6; 10:1-17). Certainly what Jesus expected them to do reveals His desire for them to be like Him.

Jesus' teaching indicates the same. Who can read the Sermon on the Mount (Matthew 5—7) and not see the character of Jesus shining through its teaching? If we live according to the Sermon, we're living like Jesus. Certainly that is what Jesus wants—for us to be like Him and live the way He did. Thus He called His disciples to make other disciples, among all peoples and in all places, who will learn and live according to His teachings (28:16-20). In other words, Jesus came, lived, died, and rose again so that the world would be filled with people who are like Him.

To make it all possible, He promised to send the Holy Spirit whose presence in our lives makes Jesus shine through. What sort of a father would ask the impossible of his children? Not a very good one. As Jesus once said, we human fathers, who could never win a Nobel prize for goodness, still know how to give good things to our children. How much more will our Heavenly Father give good things to His children (7:11)? We may safely conclude: If God calls us to the great good of being and living like Jesus, then it's *possible*. We should expect to become like Jesus, to be holy, as we walk with Him. But how? I believe the key to being like Jesus is the Cross.

Take away the Cross and the story of Jesus isn't much of a story. It becomes the account of a man who wows the crowds as storyteller, moral instructor, prophet, healer, and razzle-dazzle miracle worker. The history of the world tells many such stories, some true and some not. Perhaps they offer good examples, but good examples do not help us when we need it most. When we lose our jobs, struggle in our marriages, watch the kids make bad choices, feel bad about something we've done, or worry about the future, how do mere examples help?

Jesus said about himself, "The Son of Man must undergo great suffering, . . . be killed, and on the third day be raised [to life]" (Luke 9:22, NRSV). Why? To show the world God's love and forgiveness. And He challenged further, "If any want to become my followers, let them deny themselves and take up their cross daily and follow me" (9:23, NRSV).

So the key to being like Jesus and being holy is this—embracing the Cross. Let me describe three ways we embrace the Cross as we follow Jesus on the way of holy living.

As the Measure of God's Love

How do we *know* when it's love—real, deep love coming our way, especially when the lover is God? God's answer to the question is the cross of Jesus.

This is how God showed his love among us: He sent his one and only Son into the world that we might live through him. This is love: not that we loved God, but that he loved us and sent his Son as an atoning sacrifice for our sins *(1 John 4:9-12)*.

What does it do to us to realize that God gave His Son to die for us? Has that fact become so familiar that it no longer moves us? In the Cross, we see the most impressive display of God's love for us. When that love flows into our hearts, it motivates us to share it, to let our lives be channels through which His love can flow to others.

As the Way of Forgiveness

How wonderful to know we are forgiven! Some time ago, one of our three daughters came home from school and was unusually quiet. Obviously, something was wrong. When her mom asked about her day, she began to cry. In class that day the students took a quiz, exchanged papers with a neighbor, and corrected them before handing them in. On an impulse, our daughter had changed a wrong answer to make it right. She knew better, and as the day wore on, she felt worse and worse. By suppertime, it had become unbearable. "It feels so bad," she sobbed.

Immediately, Mom scooped her up, held her gently, and explained: "Jesus is talking to you. You've done something wrong, and the only thing that will make it better is to ask Jesus to forgive you"—which she promptly did.

Later that same evening, she exclaimed, "Mommy, I feel all new inside!"

When we do something wrong, consequences always follow. What happens in a little girl's tender heart should happen in all of us. Wrongdoing *should* make us feel bad. That's the way God made us.

The culture around us pretends we can get away with it. There are no consequences. The world of TV and cinema especially champions this view. When people drop like flies in the spray of a machine gun, how often do we see the broken-hearted family that may never heal from the wounds? The next time we watch a flirtation lead to attraction and then adultery, ask about the spouses and kids at home. Where are they, and what are they doing? What will they do when the truth hits home? The media might portray their work as reflecting life in the real world, but truth without consequences always fails a "reality check."

When we embrace the cross of Jesus, we're admitting what the world denies. There *is* a price to pay, and there *are* consequences. We have suffered brokenness in our relationships with God, others, and ourselves because we have not been right. We've been wrong.

Jesus hung on the Cross as a consequence of *our* sin. In His dying, He assumed those consequences. Embracing the Cross means we accept this fact about ourselves, owning up to who we are and how we've lived. We claim nothing in God's presence and can do nothing to make up for our sin. In our brokenness and emptiness, we can only appeal to God to do something. By embracing and clinging to the Cross, we accept Jesus' death for us as God's offer of forgiveness and pardon.

There's a bumper sticker I sometimes see that I don't like. It reads, "I'm not perfect, just forgiven." I don't like it for two reasons. First, it suggests I'm supposed to be perfect, and that's not true. While the Bible uses terms sometimes translated with words like "perfect," the original terms do not mean what we understand as "perfection." The biblical terms refer to reaching the goal God intends for us and becoming mature in Christ. Nowhere are we told to be flawless or to perform with absolute precision and consistency. That sort of perfection belongs only to God.

Second, I don't like this bumper sticker because it suggests that being "just forgiven" is a small thing. Being merely forgiven provides an excuse for something not right in my life. That also is not true.

When God forgives us, things change. We have a new re-

lationship with God, the Creator and eternal Lord. We are OK
with Him. If we're OK with the Creator God, then we're OK—
period! If He can forgive us, we can forgive ourselves. We can
stop beating ourselves up over what should or could have
been. Instead, God can begin to build us up and shape us into
what we should and can be.

God's forgiveness through Jesus' cross becomes the basis
for an entirely new identity. Here we find the source of a proper, healthy view of ourselves as persons. Also we find a new
foundation for relating to other people in our lives.

Indeed, if God can forgive us, we can forgive others.
Their sins against us cannot be excused anymore than our sins
can be. Neither can others deal with their sins anymore than
we could handle ours. Only God can deal with sin and its
consequences. If God can do it for us, He can also do it for
others. When we embrace the Cross, we will want God to
have His way with all sin and wrong—ours and theirs. So we
let God have it all. We trust God to do what only God can do.
Just as we have sighed in relief and cried in praise because
God has forgiven us and made us right, so we wait to see how
God will work in the lives of people who have wronged us.
Embracing the Cross means walking on the way of forgiveness, delighting in our own forgiveness, and forgiving others
in hopes that they will one day share the same delight.

As the Way to Freedom

Why do we need forgiveness in the first place? Why do
we find it hard to forgive others? Even after we have received
God's forgiveness, why is it we sometimes find ourselves not
right and not doing the right thing?

By nature, we are self-centered creatures. We want what
we want when we want it. If it's good for *us*, it's good. Certainly we are more subtle and sophisticated than these blunt as-
sertions would suggest. Nevertheless, sort it all out, and at the
root of all that is not right with us is an obsessive, slavish concern for self. Spot a marriage in trouble, a shady business deal,

a strained friendship, an unjust social system, a war, or a starving population and a slavish concern for self can be spotted somewhere at work. What about *me?* Where's *mine?* Why *me?* These are the operative questions we ask.

How hard it is—impossible in fact—to have a balanced home, a close friendship, a deep satisfaction about life when we're constantly worried about ourselves. What a burden and hassle it is!

Jesus invites us to embrace the Cross, to deny ourselves and follow Him. We know Jesus was saying precisely this because in the next breath He explained: "For those who want to save their life will lose it, and those who lose their life for my sake will save it" (Luke 9:24, NRSV).

The Cross signals God's offer to deliver us from self-centered living. The apostle Paul takes up Jesus' invitation and explains how it works:

> "I have been crucified with Christ and I no longer live, but Christ lives in me. The life I live in the body, I live by faith in the Son of God, who loved me and gave himself for me" *(Galatians 2:20).*

What does this mean? Quite simply, when we begin to follow Jesus, embracing the Cross, we die to one way of life—the old way dominated by selfishness—so that we may live in a new way. In other words, in shouldering the Cross, followers of Jesus are free to live like Jesus. Again Paul explains:

> Don't you know that all of us who were baptized into Christ Jesus were baptized into his death? We were therefore buried with him through baptism into death in order that, just as Christ was raised from the dead . . . we too may live a new life *(Romans 6:3-4).*

In this "new life," God has already set us free from sinful slavery to self.

> For we know that our old self was crucified with him so that the body of sin might be [rendered powerless], that we should no longer be slaves to sin—because anyone who has died has been freed from sin *(vv. 6-7).*

What should we do with our new freedom?

> Put to death, therefore, whatever belongs to your earthly nature: sexual immorality, impurity, lust, evil desires and greed, which is idolatry . . . Now you must rid yourselves of . . . anger, rage, malice, slander, and filthy language from your lips (*Colossians 3:5-8*).

As we bring these qualities of the old life to their death on the Cross, we find a wonderful freedom to live the new life:

> Therefore, as God's chosen people, holy and dearly loved, clothe yourselves with compassion, kindness, humility, gentleness, and patience. Bear with each other and forgive whatever grievances you may have against one another. Forgive as the Lord forgave you. And over all these virtues put on love, which binds them all together in perfect unity (*vv. 12-14*).

In fact, embracing the Cross liberates us to be like Jesus, to love as He has loved, and to forgive others as He has forgiven us.

One summer several years ago, I fell desperately ill. It felt like the worst flu I'd ever had, but it went on for weeks. At first, I struggled to keep going, but finally the illness disabled me. I lay flat in bed, so nauseated that even turning from side to side was unthinkable. Eventually dehydration set in. Only ignorance (and probably a bit of stubbornness) kept me from fearing for my life.

During this time of illness, I needed to do certain things —work to provide for my family, serve my brothers and sisters in the church, help win my community to Christ. All sorts of things begged for my attention—good, worthy things. I really wanted to rejoin the living in these and other ways, but what I truly needed most was to get well.

As long as that bug—whatever it was—had its way with me, I couldn't even think about living the good life. In fact, I should have begun to think about not living at all.

What I needed most was a way to kill that bug and allow me sufficient freedom to embrace the ways of life. Thankfully, my doctor offered just what I needed—a prescription. He told me to take it, not just until I started to feel better but until there was none left to take. The medicine had to be embraced until it was completely consumed. If I stopped when I was well enough to start eating and resume minimal activity, the bug would make a comeback, and I would have a setback. If I took all my medicine, all would be well. Soon I resumed a healthy life, fulfilling my various roles with joy.

The illustration is far from perfect but still helpful. When we first embrace the Cross to follow Jesus, He frees us from a life centered on self. As Paul indicated, we buried the person we used to be. New life surges through us. However, we must take all our medicine, the *whole* prescription. We must continue to embrace the Cross as the remedy God offers for the selfish and sinful life we would otherwise live.

As I say, the illustration isn't perfect. Eventually I took all of my medicine, recovered fully, and life went on, independent of all medication. However, we never get beyond our need for the Cross. If we stop embracing it, imagining that we no longer need the power of Jesus' cross in our lives and depending on ourselves, we will revert to our former selves. We will neither love as God loves nor forgive as He forgives. Unless we continue to embrace the Cross, we will not be free to live as Jesus would live.

We Must Embrace the Cross, but How?

Years ago I was moving several heavy boxes from one part of our home to another. As always in those days, my little girl was there to "help." "Daddy," she said, "I can do that. Let *me* carry it! OK?"

I said, "OK!" It was obvious to me that she couldn't really do it, even though she really wanted to help.

So I watched with interest to see what would happen. She bent over, grabbed hold of it, and quickly realized it was much heavier than she thought. Then, just as quickly, she looked up into my eyes and said, "Daddy, will you help me? Can we do it together?"

Who really did it? Since I supplied the strength, you might say I did it. Yet, in a very real sense, she did it too. She placed her will and desire—her all—in my hands as I lifted.

That's how we embrace the Cross. Once we decide to follow Jesus, He gives us His Spirit. From that moment on, the Holy Spirit works within our lives. He shows us the Cross for what it is, He reveals our need for freedom to live as Jesus would live, and He empowers us to pick it up. Like my daughter, we may look to the Spirit and ask, "Will You help me? Can we do it together?" As we surrender our will and desire—our all—to Him, we (God and us) will do it together. And He will make us holy, like Jesus.

Background Scripture: Matthew 5—7; 10:1; 28:16-20; Mark 6:6-13; Luke 9:1-6, 22-24; 10:1-17; Romans 6:3-4, 6-7; Galatians 2:20; Colossians 3:5-8, 12-14; 1 John 4:9-12

CHAPTER 7

Living with Sacrifice

DURING THE SUMMER OF 1996, thousands of athletes and hundreds of thousands of others gathered in Atlanta for the Summer Olympic Games. What a grand event, filled with drama, deep disappointment, and exhilarating delight. During the games, athletes from around the world compete in a wide variety of athletic events. Their goal? To stand in the winner's spotlight, wearing a medal around the neck, cradling a bouquet of flowers, and listening to the familiar sounds of their national anthem.

Without exception, those who enjoyed this moment in the winner's circle had become experts at delayed gratification. For years they worked and trained, often overcoming enormous obstacles, all for a moment of ecstatic satisfaction. It was not uncommon to see tears stream down a winner's cheeks in the sheer joy of the moment. We could describe them in more common, earthy, and theological language by saying these were people who have "gutted it out" so they could get "beyond the Cross to the glory."

We have seen that the holy life means being like Jesus, following Jesus so closely that, as we walk in His footsteps, we become like Him. We've also seen that the key to being like Jesus is embracing the Cross. That's the way really to live, according to Jesus, and to be holy.

Then what? Having embraced the Cross, we anticipate glory, right? Doesn't it seem correct to suppose that we eventually get beyond the Cross, leaving all that unpleasantness behind, to grab a bit of glory? Don't we feel just like that when we pass through periods of brokenness and difficulty? "I'll bear the Cross, the Lord being my helper," we say, "but I can't wait to be done with it!" If, however, we watch Jesus closely and listen to Him carefully, we will learn that the Cross isn't like that.

Followers of Jesus Never Get Beyond the Cross

We must not understand the Cross as a necessary evil we embrace in order to move quickly to the glory of a "resurrection life." That is not an option for us because Jesus didn't understand the Cross in such terms. In fact, Jesus offered cross-bearing as *the* model for discipleship, for an entire life of following Him. "Let them . . . take up their cross *daily*" (Luke 9:23, NRSV, emphasis added). Since we never get beyond following Jesus, we will never get beyond carrying or bearing the Cross.

There can be no doubt that the first followers of Jesus understood Him in just this way. Chief among them was the apostle Paul, who constantly described daily Christian living in terms of the cross of Jesus. He told his Philippian friends:

> Whatever was to my profit I now consider loss for the sake of Christ. What is more, I consider everything as a loss compared to the surpassing greatness of knowing Christ Jesus my Lord, for whose sake I have lost all things. I consider them rubbish, that I may gain Christ and be found in him, not having a righteousness of my own that comes from the law, but that which is through faith in Christ—the righteousness that comes from God and is by faith. I want to know Christ and the power of his resurrection and the fellowship of sharing in his sufferings, becoming like him in his death, and so, somehow, to attain to the resurrection from the dead (3:7-11).

Paul looked forward to being in the winner's circle with Christ, being completely like Christ, and sharing in the glory of the Resurrection. Yet on the way to the winner's circle, he describes his life in terms of bearing the Cross—sharing in Christ's sufferings and being like Him in his death.

He said the same thing to the Corinthians:

We always carry around in our body the death of Jesus, so that the life of Jesus may also be revealed in our body. For we who are alive are always being given over to death for Jesus' sake, so that his life may be revealed in our mortal body *(2 Corinthians 4:10-11)*.

In other words, in order for Jesus' likeness to shine through so that no one can miss it, we live a life wrapped up in the cross of Jesus. Holy living, being like Jesus, requires cross-bearing. Paul never gets beyond the Cross.

Still, what about the resurrection and living in the power of the resurrection? Doesn't Paul, and God through him, call us to live by the power of the Resurrection? Indeed. Remember what he told the church at Rome: "We were therefore buried with him through baptism into death in order that, just as Christ was raised from the dead, . . . we too may live a new life" (6:4). God fills us with His Spirit and the power of the resurrection so that we may take up our cross daily and be like Jesus. That's what Paul meant when he wrote, "We have this treasure [the gospel and the life it gives us] in jars of clay [the frail, broken human person] to show that this all-surpassing [resurrection] power is from God and not from us" (2 Corinthians 4:7). Through Spirit-empowered cross-bearing the world can't help but notice that God is at work in our lives.

Sacrifice

Followers of Jesus live a life of sacrifice. Of course, we do—or we should. What else could Jesus' call to take up the Cross mean if not sacrifice?

That's not how we often think about faith in Jesus and following Jesus, is it? Interestingly, in the North American culture, being Christian is sometimes promoted as a way to self-fulfillment. How often have we heard talk of following Jesus as the way to happiness and the secret of success? Certainly much depends on what we mean by success and happiness. Yet, isn't it odd how we can hear Jesus' invitation to follow Him and so quickly forget the element of sacrifice? "Follow Jesus so that when you die you'll have the right answer that will admit you to heaven," we hear. "Commit to Jesus' way of life and your depression, loneliness, emotional pain, physical illness, or stalled car will be all right," we're promised.

Is it possible to follow Jesus without sacrifice? Can we take up the Cross as Jesus did without foregoing some things —whether possessions, experiences, freedoms, comforts, or conveniences? I'm not talking about bad things. Of course, following Jesus means leaving bad things behind, but that's not the point.

Here's the point: taking up the Cross, by its very nature, means sacrifice. To do it daily means a life of sacrifice. In Luke's presentation of the gospel, Jesus makes this point with special force. First, Jesus calls us to rigorous discipleship— daily cross-bearing (9:23-26). But He doesn't leave the matter there, assuming that His disciples will know what rigorous discipleship means. Instead, He proceeds to go to Jerusalem, where cross-bearing leads to death for Him. Then on the way to His appointment with the Cross, He teaches us what cross-bearing means. In fact, most of Jesus' teaching on discipleship in Luke's Gospel comes on the way to the Cross.

When you look at this teaching, it has "sacrifice" written all over it. The Good Samaritan's sacrifice meant time, energy, money, and bodily danger to help someone in need, even someone who hated him and his kind (10:25-37). For Martha, sacrifice meant setting aside social custom in order to give full attention to Jesus (10:38-42). The rich fool, who never had enough even though he had no needs, models a disdain for sacrifice that proved deadly. For him, sacrifice would have meant holding things more loosely in order to get a firm grasp on God (12:16-21). For some households, sacrifice meant choosing Jesus over loved ones and losing the benefits of family life (12:49-53).

Sacrifice for the host and guests at the banquet called for humility and a rejection of the self-seeking and status that others find perfectly acceptable, if not expected (14:1-14).

Sacrifice means counting the cost and paying the price of going the whole way with Jesus, no matter how high (14:15-34). Sacrifice for religious insiders who enjoy the security and blessings of belonging to God requires a radical openness and gracious welcome toward "unworthies" whose former life offends cultured spirituality (15:1-32). For the rich, being right with God would have led to generous care of the poor (16:19-31) or simply giving everything away to be free to follow Jesus wholly (18:18-29).

I'm not suggesting that all true disciples who really desire to be like Jesus will do all these things. Not everyone in Jesus' day, or in the life of the Early Church, assumed all these forms of sacrifice. Still, as earnest followers of Jesus, all of them were well acquainted with sacrifice. That's the point: those who seriously walk with Jesus live, give, and serve in ways that are sacrificial.

In fact, sacrifice is the norm for followers of Jesus, according to the New Testament. Often, however, we think of sacrifice as the exception rather than the norm. And it's no wonder. Sacrifice is hard, and who likes hard? Where's the fun in that? Invite people to sacrifice, and we'd better prepare for loneliness! Who would become a Christian these days, or stay one, if we insisted that the way of Christ is a way of sacrifice?

Yet these questions merit close attention. On the surface, people seem to prefer avoiding sacrifice at all costs. At a deeper level, however, most of us are highly attracted to sacrifice. Let me explain.

I love to hear and watch gifted musicians—whether the great masters of classical music or the newer varieties of musical genius. I could be wrong, and I suspect there are exceptions, but hardly any gifted musicians were born with their expertise. The vast majority of them sacrificed to acquire their skill, develop their talent, and have continued to sacrifice in order to bless those who hear them. I find that sort of sacrifice incredibly attractive!

We live in a town that is crazy for basketball. Our high

school boys' team has made a habit of winning the state championship tournament each year. We are so accustomed to their "winning it all" that a second-place finish no longer merits a celebration. Yet, none of those young basketball champions could enjoy such triumph without all kinds of sacrifice along the way. For most of them, the sacrifices began in early elementary school.

All Olympic champions enjoyed their moment in the winner's circle only on the strength of a whole lifetime of sacrifice. I'm drawn by the prospects of that sort of sacrifice. Aren't we all?

Truth to tell, we can't even grow a garden without sacrifice (and some of us can't under *any* circumstances). Most communities find their beauty enhanced by the green thumbs of their members but not without the considerable care and labor that spell sacrifice.

Each spring we celebrate the graduations of high school and college students. There could be no parties without sacrifice.

I think we all know deep down that the best things in life simply do not happen apart from sacrifice. I confess, I'm attracted to and eager to see the best things. How wonderful are the sacrifices that make them possible!

Now look still deeper for another surprise. Not only are most of us attracted to sacrifice, but also most of us are now, or have been, deeply committed to sacrifice as essential to our lives. How could we have received the education we did, or the work we have, or the help we've needed along the way without sacrifice—our own and that of others? How could we raise our children and send them into the world as mature disciples of Jesus without making some sacrifices along the way? The truth is this: if we ever accomplished anything or did anything well, it happened because we made any number of sacrifices in order to learn, practice, and develop. Probably all of us have sacrificed money, time, energy, privileges, and other things in order to pursue some goal to accomplishment.

So the question is not whether we live a life of sacrifice. The question is what are our goals? What is our aim in life? What are we truly pursuing? What is supremely important to us? Answer these questions seriously, and we'll find ourselves making all kinds of sacrifices along the way.

Obviously, insignificant or trivial things do not call for sacrifice, but important things always do. Therefore, we shouldn't be surprised if sharing in the kingdom of God and being like the Son of God means sacrificial living.

Let's be clear: we're not called to sacrifice in order to be acceptable before God. *Nothing* except God's love offered to us in Jesus' death can give us new life. Only what *God* does for us makes us acceptable in His presence.

God has no interest in making us trophies or cute little monuments to His goodness. He aims to make us His people. He calls us to be like Jesus. That aim of God, when taken earnestly, always leads to sacrifice.

Jesus' followers become Olympic in their desires and efforts at following Him and pursuing His goals. With World Series earnestness, they invest their time and energy in Jesus' name for Jesus' cause. Their date books and calendars suggest radical commitment to following Jesus. With World Cup zeal, they make their possessions available to bless others, to be used so others will know God's love and develop into Jesus-like people. When they do their taxes on their personal computers, the software auditing function questions their contributions to the church and charities because they give so much.

Jesus' followers pursue God's best for others with championship passion. People who know them can't believe their openness and concern, their willingness to listen and share, and their eagerness to demonstrate Jesus' way of dealing with life.

Jesus' followers join the apostle Paul in saying, "One thing I do: Forgetting what is behind and straining toward what is ahead, I press on toward the goal to win the prize for which God has called me heavenward in Christ Jesus" (Philippians 3:13-14). The sacrifice of straining, stretching, and pressing on conditions all they are, all they have, and all they do.

A friend of mine pastors a Mennonite church near our town. Some time ago, he told me about a guest speaker who recently visited his church. He was a man from Zaire, Africa, now the Democratic Republic of Congo. This man had come to share recent happenings in Central African Mennonite Missions.

As they drove from the airport to the church, my friend the pastor asked his guest if he had ever heard of Larry Kauffman. Larry was a man who had gone as a missionary to Zaire from my friend's congregation more than 40 years ago. He served there for just a short time, however, before dying in a drowning accident.

At the mention of Larry Kauffman's name, the African's face lit up as he said, "I didn't know Larry was from here! Yes, I knew him rather well!" Then he went on to tell of the impact of this missionary's life and death among them.

Through the missionary's death, the church in Zaire came to understand that following Jesus meant willingness to go halfway around the world and, if necessary, die. What blessing this missionary's life of sacrifice had brought to thousands in Zaire.

Let me confess, as I consider God's call to be like Jesus, I have a twofold reaction. First, from deep within me there is a yearning, a longing that cries out "Yes!" This is what I truly desire—to be like Jesus and to make a difference in the world by following Him.

There's also a second response. It's a kind of nagging question. What does this life of sacrifice mean for me? It's not really a guilt trip but a continuing quest to find answers to that question and shape my life accordingly. It's a question I want to ask in relation to the use of time, money, and energy. It's a question I use to evaluate the status quo of my comfortable life, family, and church. The question surfaces when I see what's going on elsewhere in the world and even in my own backyard. It's a question that often unsettles me.

Yet it's a good question because, through asking it, God's Spirit draws me closer to Jesus and to His likeness. This yearning to be like Jesus, whatever it takes, comes from the Lord. As with all God-given desires, the Spirit will work to make it so.

Background Scripture: Luke 9:23-26; 10:25-42; 12:16-21, 49-53; 14:1-34; 15:1-32; 16:19-31; 18:18-29; Romans 6:4; 2 Corinthians 4:7, 10-11; Philippians 3:7-11, 13-14

CHAPTER 8

Accepting the Mantle of Servanthood

WHEN WE ENCOUNTER GOD, who is holy, soon we find ourselves serving. We've recalled the experience of Isaiah the prophet. Once God met his need, the prophet was ready to say, "Here am I. Send me!" (6:8). Likewise, when Peter recognized Jesus as the Holy One, Jesus called him to a different kind of fishing (Luke 5:10).

Of course, Jesus himself models the sort of ministry to which holiness always leads. In his letter to the Philippians, Paul reminded them that the whole life of Jesus could be told in terms of humble, obedient service. Probably he's citing a poem or hymn when he describes Jesus:

Who, being in very nature God, did not consider equality with God something to be grasped, but made himself nothing, taking the very nature of a servant, being made in human likeness. And being found in appearance as a man, he humbled himself and became obedient to death—even death on a cross! (2:6-8).

Paul cites this remarkable account of Jesus' life in order to explain what it means to have the same "attitude . . . as that of Christ Jesus" (2:5). Indeed, if holiness means to be like Jesus, then it means being a servant.

In John's Gospel, we find a moving story of how Jesus modeled servanthood (13:1-17). It happened during supper the night before the Crucifixion. Surprisingly, Jesus rose from the table, where He was recognized as the Master, Teacher, and Lord. Then He began to act like the lowest slave—the sort of slave few would notice, a slave with no real identity, reduced to a common, lowly function.

What Jesus Did

First, He interrupted the meal. The food was on the table, and they'd all begun to eat, but Jesus got up from His place at the table. Jesus' time was slipping away and permitted only the most important words and deeds. What Jesus was about to do was more important than eating and celebrating the holiday.

Then He washed their feet. Foot washing was a common way of showing respect to a guest, especially to an honored guest, though ordinarily only a slave would perform this service. Jesus identified with the lowest of the low when He stripped to the waist, wrapped the towel around himself, and took the basin to each pair of feet.

He was breaking most of the rules of social grace and protocol. People of His stature and status simply didn't do such things. Jesus turned everything upside down by taking up the towel and basin. He wanted to show them, and us, no one is unworthy of being served and no one is too important to serve.

When Jesus finished washing their feet and returned to the table, He asked His disciples, "Do you understand?" (13:12). Not waiting for their answer, He told them, "I'm the Teacher and Lord. Now let Me teach you. Let Me show you the way, the only way. I've just given you an example of how My people relate to others. If this is what *I* do, this is what *you* should do" (vv. 13-15, author's paraphrase).

Putting Jesus' Lesson into Practice
Doug

In 1967 Doug Nichols served in India with a Christian relief organization. Unfortunately, however, shortly after his term of service began, he came down with tuberculosis. Even worse, the only means of treatment open to him required several months in a sanitarium for TB patients. So there he was—sick and disappointed, among fellow patients, doctors, nurses, and hospital staff whose language he did not speak or read.

Since Doug was a Christian, committed to sharing Christ wherever he was, he determined to serve the Lord in that place. As strength allowed, he gave out tracts telling about Jesus. He noted that the people received the papers with a smile but later threw them into the trash. What a sense of failure he felt!

Then one night, things began to change. Doug awoke at 2 A.M. with a fit of coughing. Just as he calmed down, he noticed an older and sicker man across the room trying to get out of bed. He would sit up, inch toward the edge, and try to stand, only to fall back into bed, crying softly. The next morning Doug realized what the man was trying to do—simply go to the bathroom. Soon everyone knew about it, as the terrible stench of his accident quickly spread throughout the ward. Other patients and even the staff yelled at the man and abused him for the mess he had made.

The next night it was the same story. The man tried, but couldn't get up, and fell back into bed whimpering.

Doug will tell you he hates bad smells and really didn't want to get involved. Still, he approached the man's bed, looked into his frightened eyes, and gained silent permission to pick him up. He carried the man to the room where there was just a hole in the ground and held him up while he took care of himself. When Doug returned the man to his bed, the man said something he didn't understand and kissed him on the cheek.

The next morning another patient came over and offered Doug a steaming cup of tea. Then he began to make motions until Doug realized he was asking for one of those gospel tracts. Throughout the day, others also came and asked for the little booklet that told about Jesus.

Later Doug learned that a number of people eventually decided to follow Jesus, but not because they found the tracts so persuasive. It was because Doug had followed the example of Jesus by taking that trip to the bathroom.[1]

Jesus said, "I have set you an example that you should do as I have done" (John 13:15).

Don

I first met Don when we were both students in seminary. We became friends but drifted apart after graduation, eventually losing all contact. Then out of the blue, he called my name at a large conference I attended several years ago. It had been 15 years, but neither of us had changed so much as to be unrecognizable to the other.

Don told me God had called him to be a church planter in the South. Remarkably, over the last several years he had seen one church begin, grow to about 250 regular attendees, and then spin off a daughter congregation. Then another and another. At the time of our meeting, they were working on the fourth church plant.

One of their key strategies for letting folk in the community know they are followers of Jesus especially caught my attention. They organized teams of two or three who make themselves available to perform services no one else is likely to do. For example, armed with rubber gloves and cleaning supplies, they visit area restaurants, businesses, or recreation centers and ask if they can clean the bathrooms. When they hear the inevitable question, "Why do you want to clean our toilets?" they answer, "Because we are followers of Jesus!"

Kevin

Kevin Miller, editor of *Leadership* magazine, told about his father, who had passed away several years before. Mr. Miller had been an important man, a vice president at Harper-Row Publishers. In one of Kevin's most vivid memories, his dad came into the room, saying, "Come on, kid. Let's go."

"Where to?" Kevin asked.

"Lucy's!"

Once a month Mr. Miller visited Lucy, a woman whose

body had been twisted and pinned to a wheelchair by arthritis. During those visits, he would pick up her frail body out of the chair, place her in the front seat of the car, fold the chair, put it in the trunk, and take her for a drive. Here was a VIP shuttling a shut-in, because Jesus said, "I have set you an example" (13:15).[2]

Caroling

Every year during Advent, we have an all-church "caroling and chili" event. We gather in the fellowship hall, organize into minichoirs, and go caroling, especially visiting people who are homebound. Then after making the rounds, we return to the church to enjoy piping hot chili.

One year, Lavone and I led a group to a care facility in town. Up and down the halls we roamed, serving the residents by bringing them a hearty dose of Christmas cheer. On one of our stops we were near the room of a lady who eagerly rolled her wheelchair to the door to see and hear us sing. As we sang "Joy to the World," I noticed a young lady in our group stooping to help this dear woman recover the slipper she had lost in wheeling her chair to the hallway. Most of us didn't even notice the need, but this young lady did and met it. By far, the most notable thing about our visit was not our singing but this act of attentive care.

What Jesus Wants

Quite simply, Jesus calls us to be servants as He was. Now, having called us, He wants to make it so.

If you're like me, in all honesty, you are both attracted and repulsed by what Jesus wants us to do. On the one hand, what beautiful and moving stories can be told about people who serve the way Jesus did. The beauty of these stories and the wonderful impact such service has on people's lives draws us toward Jesus-style service.

On the other hand, most of us are not greatly attracted to feet, toilets, and wheelchairs. Nor do we automatically get excited about spending time and energy in such service when we never seem to have enough of these as it is.

We're not so sure about being on the other end either. Do we really want other people washing our feet or otherwise stepping in to help us? Do we even want others to know when and where we have needs? Attracted and repulsed!

Well, there's "good news and bad news." The bad news is that Jesus doesn't give us options at this point. He doesn't simply offer a suggestion for us to consider. He tells Peter, "Unless you let me do this for you, you can't have anything to do with me" (John 13:8, author's paraphrase). Then He tells all of them, "I have set you an example that you should do as I have done for you" (v. 15). That is, followers of Jesus will routinely find themselves on both ends of "towel and basin" service.

Here's the good news: we don't become servants like Jesus on our own. We may hear His call and desire to say yes, but unless He first "serves" us, we will never be able to serve others as He did.

Of course, Jesus is eager to serve us in this way. Remember the setting of the foot washing. It was just before Passover. Recall that Jesus is the Lamb of God, sacrificed to take away the sin of the world. His sacrifice makes us alive and free the way Jesus was.

Jesus wants to free us to use our powers, our abilities, resources, and energies to serve others. We don't have to be insecure and thus always grasping for control. Nor do we need to hang on tightly to what we have for fear of losing it.

Jesus wants to free us to serve—even to be kind, considerate, and helpful toward the enemy. Remember that one pair of the feet Jesus washed belonged to Judas.

Jesus wants to free us to develop servant eyes that see how we may be helpful and servant hearts that will move us to help.

Jesus would also like to free us so that we can receive the service of others. He would make His followers a community of mutual serving. To accomplish His plan He would cleanse

away the pride and self-consciousness that keeps us from
serving others and from allowing others to serve us.

I suspect that most of us travel in similar circles when it
comes to serving and being served. We'd much rather be on
the serving end of things. I've had several friends through the
years much wealthier than I. Do you think they ever let me
pick up the check when we have lunch together? Not on your
life! At least, not without a great deal of urging and sometimes
sneaking around on my part. Certainly they mean well, and I
deeply appreciate their generosity. But as I've tried to explain
on several occasions, when I say, "Please, let me treat this
time," it really would be a treat for me. It feels good to give!
They do me a favor by letting me serve them.

Who pays for lunch probably won't count for eternity,
but the hesitancy to let other people serve us may have pro-
found consequence. Think about the persons facing serious
needs. A suspicious shadow on the X ray requires some diag-
nostic tests or exploratory surgery. A child makes a poor
choice, leaving parents grief stricken. A work situation creates
mile-high anxiety. A company's downsizing threatens a family's
security. In each of these situations, and hundreds like them, a
refusal to be served hurts both those who would love to serve
in Jesus' name and those who would be helped by receiving.
In addition, a hesitancy to let others serve us robs the church
family of an opportunity to show an unbelieving world what
following Jesus really means. That's what Jesus wants—to
show the world His love through us as a community of mutual servants.

If this is what Jesus wants to do for us, then how, in fact,
does He do it? I'm sure that if Jesus could literally walk beside us
in our daily lives, we wouldn't ask this question. In each situation we enter, Jesus would show us the way. If His signals
weren't clear, we could ask Him to clarify His will. Of course,
that's impossible. Jesus can't literally walk beside every one of us.

Yet, He can do something even better. At least, Jesus said
it was better (see John 16:7). He promised to send His disci-

ples the Holy Spirit, to be a companion to them in the way Jesus was, minus the obvious limitations that go with physical presence. Even more, He said the Spirit would be within His disciples to reveal and make clear the way of Jesus and empower them to walk on that way.

He promised the Spirit's presence within us. He kept His word, and He gave us His Spirit. In ways we cannot fully understand, much less explain, the Spirit lives within us. If we ask the Spirit to accomplish Jesus' plan in us and through us, we may be sure He will. As He cleanses us and empowers us to follow Jesus, He makes us servants and holy.

Background Scripture: Isaiah 6:8; Luke 5:10; John 13:1-17; 16:7; Philippians 2:5-8

---

1. *Leadership,* spring 1994, 94.
2. *Leadership,* winter 1996, 3.

CHAPTER 9

Understanding the Mission of Jesus

WE ARE, AFTER ALL, followers of Jesus, and Jesus was on a mission. In Luke's Gospel, Jesus announced His mission shortly after He began His public life:

> The Spirit of the Lord is on me, because he has anointed me to preach good news to the poor. He has sent me to proclaim freedom for the prisoners and recovery of sight for the blind, to release the oppressed, to proclaim the year of the Lord's favor *(4:18-19)*.

Jesus went on to tell the people that His ministry would fulfill these prophetic words. Then in the rest of the Gospel, He accepts and accomplishes this divine mission. The rest of the Gospel story also shows us that following Jesus means accepting *His* mission as *ours*.

Actually, the holiness of Jesus' followers—the difference between them and other people—can perhaps be seen most clearly at the point of mission. Most other organizations have the benefits of its members most in mind. The church is one of the few organizations that exist for the sake of its nonmembers. At the heart of it all, that difference expresses our mission as the holy people of God.

I've tried to imagine, plan, and implement what it means for the church—the people of God—truly to exist for others. Certainly no less than a complete change of attitude and orientation is often required among the people, as a whole church and as various classes and groups within the church.

Sociologists claim that most of us have from six to eight people right around us whom we could influence for Jesus. What
would happen if the classes and small groups of our churches
began to ask, Who are these people close to us? What makes
them tick? What are their needs and hurts? What would God
like to do in their lives? How could we help God accomplish
His will for them? Then suppose we not only asked such
questions but let them set the agenda for the church's programs and ministries. I think we'd be preparing ourselves for
exciting days in mission!

The Mission

By "mission" I don't mean going to Africa or some other
exotic place. Nor do I refer to moving into an urban center to
work in a soup kitchen. And I don't mean becoming a pastor.
Of course, "mission" *could* mean any or all of these. I would
encourage any and all serious followers of Jesus to consider
such options!

Rather, I'm using "mission" to describe our orientation
and perspective in life. Mission speaks to the sense of purpose
we have as we make our way through life following Jesus.
Mission refers to the destiny that is rooted in our identity as
people of God.

Aliens

In 1 Peter we find special insight into our mission as holy
people. To begin, Peter used two very interesting words to describe Christian people. He called them "strangers" (1:1; 2:11)
and "aliens" (2:11). Those terms usually described people either passing through foreign territory or temporarily living in
a foreign country. Almost always some calamity had forced
them from their homes to foreign soil—famine, plague, war,
or some other catastrophe. Visiting "strangers" and resident
"aliens" also described the social and cultural situations of
these people. To be a stranger or alien meant not belonging,
even if they'd settled down, built a home, and found work.

Since they lacked native or citizen status, they were denied the rights and privileges that others around them enjoyed. For that reason, they would likely suffer at least mild forms of discrimination, if not blatant persecution.

Peter used these terms to describe the situation of Christians in the world. God has made them a new and different kind of people and for that reason they live the life of aliens and strangers. In other words, Christians do not belong here in this world but somewhere else. Ultimately, they do not trace their roots to others in this world but to God.

The apostle Paul made the same point in his Philippians letter. "Our citizenship is in heaven. And we eagerly await a Savior from there, the Lord Jesus Christ" (3:20). Likewise, the writer of Hebrews celebrated the faithful of old as models for our life of faith:

By faith Abraham, when called . . . obeyed and went, even though he did not know where he was going. By faith he made his home in the promised land like a stranger in a foreign country . . . All these people were still living by faith when they died. They did not receive the things promised, they only saw them and welcomed them from a distance. And they admitted that they were aliens and strangers on earth (*Hebrews 11:8-13*).

Such imagery reminds us that belonging to God and to God's kingdom affects everything about us: What work we do and, even more, how we do it. The people we associate with, and the people with whom we establish deep friendships. The one we marry and those we date before we marry. What we do with our time. How we spend our money. How and what we plan for the future. Not belonging to the world and belonging to God makes us different or holy.

As I write this, I'm reminded of thousands of Christians from Rwanda in central Africa. In 1993, long-standing tribal conflict erupted into a campaign of "ethnic cleansing" as the ruling minority Tutsis sought to wipe out members of the majority Hutu tribe. Rwandan Christians fled to neighboring

Zaire and Tanzania. As "aliens," they survived in refugee camps. Yet despite all their losses—home, possessions, family members—these Christian refugees organized themselves as the people of God. Even in a land where they didn't belong, they remained the Church. Ultimately, their identity was not rooted here in this world but in God. They modeled powerfully what Peter says is true of all God's people.

Dare we ask about ourselves? How at home are we in this world? The question is not so much what we say or claim, but what does our lifestyle actually suggest about whether we've planted roots in this world or in God? Consider, if the stock market totally crashed and our economy lay in ruins, what then? If we're passed over for the promotion, how about that? If our sons and daughters leave town to be missionaries halfway around the world, what will we do? If the government revokes the tax deduction for charitable contributions, what happens to our ministry budgets? If we were driven from our native soil, would we establish the church as one of the first orders of business?

Even if we are aliens and don't belong in this world, still we spend a good bit of time here. So why are we here? Why doesn't God whisk us to heaven where we belong the moment we believe?

Family

Again, the answer is that we are followers of Jesus. God is at work to make us like Jesus as we follow Him. Jesus had a mission, and so do we.

One facet of our mission is to form a place, to *be* a place, for people to be family. How desperately our world needs this. Loneliness, brokenness, and isolation often invade modern life. Economic crisis and unemployment routinely forces people to live on the street. Spouse and child abuse leaves its victims wounded and hurting. Restlessness or dissatisfaction prompts multiple career changes, and households move here and there. Family life breaks down with epidemic frequency through divorce or lifestyle choices that drive a wedge between parents and children. These and other features of modern life hinder many people from developing deep and satisfying relationships. Closer than we know are people who need a place, a community, a family where they can be at home.

Therefore, if we take our mission seriously, we will develop and experience church as the family of God. Our churches will be home for people whose experiences in the world have left them physically, emotionally, and spiritually homeless.

I think that at least two agenda items suggest themselves for the church. First, we must make sure that we *are*, in fact, family, that our fellowship *is* fellowship. We must take care that our programs, ministries, and the mood or climate of our people communicate a welcome feel. In some cases, this may be accomplished simply by directing and shaping what is already happening in the church. Yet underneath this climate of loving acceptance must be vital spiritual reality. The church must recognize this as the true mark of the church and seek the grace to be authentic at this point. A good test for us is to observe what happens when members fall on hard times because of a lay-off, sickness, disability, or something else. Family will be there for its own and will help, even to the point of sacrifice. A second test is to ask whether the church would offer such care even to those not yet on the inside.

There's a second agenda item for the church as the family of God. The fellowship of the church as a whole and each of the church's subgroupings can become intentional about identifying the "homeless" (in every sense of the word) in the surrounding community. Who are they? What are their specific needs? How can we offer the family they need? Then, the church can design whatever ministries are needed. These ministries may be cooperative ventures with other churches or organizations. Perhaps they will even form partnerships with government agencies, locally and nationally. The current social climate almost guarantees that the ranks of the poor among us will increase in the next several decades. The church's mission as family couldn't be more relevant.

Priesthood

Peter expresses the same twofold mission in other terms: "But you are a chosen people, a royal priesthood, a holy nation, a people belonging to God, that you may declare the praises of him who called you out of darkness into his wonderful light" (1 Peter 2:9). When we come to Jesus and follow Him, we become God's special, holy people, who belong completely to Him. That's the *inward* thrust of our mission—to be a holy family. We are His people, not simply for our pleasure but for His purposes—to make Him and His plan known to others. That's the *outward* thrust of our mission—to be a holy priesthood.

This vision of our life together as holy people calls us to consider carefully how we relate to one another as fellow believers and to the world around us. Indeed, taking what Peter says seriously challenges us deeply. We are called to be the family of God. For us, that calling must be the starting point for any talk of "family values." Our first sense of belonging, after our relationship with God, should be the belonging we sense with one another as brothers and sisters in Christ. That belonging is primary for us.

What about our responsibility to the biological families God has given us? Does Jesus call us to ignore them? Jesus listed among the rigorous demands of discipleship, "If anyone comes to me and does not hate his father and mother, his wife and children, his brothers and sisters—yes, even his own life —he cannot be my disciple" (Luke 14:26). Of course, Jesus' point is *not* that we are actually to hate our loved ones or despise ourselves. Rather, our commitment to follow Him must take priority over every other commitment in this life. Aren't these demands of Jesus dangerous, especially in our Western culture where many homes suffer abuse and all kinds of dysfunction? Doesn't this reading of the cost of discipleship conflict with other clear teachings from the Scriptures? After all, in both Old and New Testaments we are commanded to take special responsibility for our biological families. (See Deuteronomy 6:1-9; Ephesians 6:4.)

Several observations have helped me sort out these matters. First, I recall that Jesus took special care of His own mother. From the Cross, He committed her care to His beloved disciple (see John 19:26-27). Obviously, then, being like Jesus and being the family of God will not lead us to abandon or refuse loving care to our families. Second, in both Testaments, family units were not regarded as separated from, but part of, the larger community of God's people. The commands to nurture and care for family always have full participation in the people of God as its goal. Certainly, the most important responsibility we have to our individual family members is to encourage their entrance into God's family. Thus, third, Jesus does not call for less family; He calls for more family. Jesus would draw us into larger and deeper family connection than would ever be possible on merely human terms. In fact, though following Jesus may lead to the loss of family in some sense, He promised 100 percent more in mothers and fathers and brothers and sisters in *this* life (see Mark 10:29-30). Jesus' call does not diminish family life; it expands and enriches it.

Yet, as we've seen, our mission to be family as the people of God does challenge us to belong so fully to God that we actually exist not for ourselves, or for our own (including our biological family), but for God and others. Exclusive relationships with our individual families and friends and the busyness of our lives that requires neglect of family (and church) signal our *un*holiness. Instead, we are called to deep involvement in one another's lives, to a kind of sharing and caring that will have a family feel to it, and to a spirit of oneness that will attract others to the family. Our mission requires us to make adjustments so that we are, in fact, the spiritual household God wants us to be.

In truth, our mission to be a priesthood—to help others make connection with God—depends on our being the family God calls us to be. When God forms us into family, we reflect the beauty, order, and love for which broken and hurting people long. If we accept our mission to be family, all sorts of people will be drawn to what they see among us. And what we tell them about God will have convincing power.

Conclusion

These three images—alien, family, and priesthood—show us that following Jesus draws us together as a new kind of people who live in the world, not for ourselves but for God and others. *Internally,* we allow God to make us family. We share together the joys and sorrows of life. We care for one another in times of need. We become a people among whom the living God beautifully dwells. *Externally,* we are eager to show and tell others what God has done for us. We penetrate the world to find, welcome, and embrace hurting and lost people who need the healing and health that only comes by being at home with God.

I recall again the thousands of Christian refugees driven from their homes in Rwanda to neighboring countries. Many of them had lost everything but life itself. Yet they had found one another in their exile and reorganized themselves as the family of God. In one of their letters to the United States, a group of these refugee brothers and sisters thanked the American church for their love and prayers during their exile. Then they requested that special offerings be taken to meet several of their most pressing needs. They asked for Bibles, hymnals, chalkboards, and sound systems. That seems like a strange wish list for people in their situation, but not really. They are God's holy people, and they have a mission. Having established their sense of family in the Spirit, now they've turned their attention to the thousands around them who need to know about Jesus. They are aliens, God's spiritual household, and a holy priesthood. Together they demonstrate and declare what God can do for all people.

Background Scripture: Deuteronomy 6:1-9; Mark 10:29-30; Luke 4:18-19; 14:26; John 19:26-27; Ephesians 6:4; Philippians 3:20; Hebrews 11:8-13; 1 Peter 1:1; 2:9, 11

CHAPTER 10

Accomplishing the Mission of Jesus

A HOLY PEOPLE can accomplish their mission from God only by working together. We cannot be the family of God by ourselves and cannot be a holy priesthood in isolation from one another. That does not mean we have no individual responsibilities in carrying out the mission. In fact, Peter insists we will never become the people God calls us to be nor fulfill our mission without tending to our individual responsibilities. He summarizes them as follows:

> Dear friends, I urge you, as aliens and strangers in the world, to abstain from sinful desires, which war against your soul. Live such good lives among the pagans that, though they accuse you of doing wrong, they may see your good deeds and glorify God on the day he visits us (1 Peter 2:11-12).

Peter tells us what we must do as "aliens and strangers in the world." He urges each of us to accept a twofold mandate that speaks to the inner (family) and outer (priesthood) thrust of our mission. First, he calls us to "abstain" or stay away from sinful desires. Most modern people do not like negatives or prohibitions. We'd like to find a positive way to say it or not say it at all, especially when it comes to spiritual matters. Still, some prohibitions simply must be heard. We tell our children not to touch the burners on the stove. We expect companies to warn us of any dangers associated with the products they make. Peter warns us about sinful desires and tells us to reject them.

We all have desires, longings, and appetites. God made us that way. Most of our desires are not sinful or wrong as such, but all of them can be perverted and twisted toward sinful ends. I suppose most of us think of sexual desire as the most common example of this. God created us as sexual beings. Therefore, not only is sexuality not wrong, it is positively right and good! Human sexuality played an important role in the original creation that God called "very good" (Genesis 1:31). But sexual desire may become sinful—and often does. I think this is because sexuality is one of God's most wonderful gifts, and our enemy takes delight in ruining it. The greater the gift and the greater the joy it brings us the more delight Satan takes in perverting it and us in the process. That's why holiness language in the Bible is often used in relation to sexuality. By attacking us at the point of sexual desire, the enemy hopes to rob us of God's good gift and keep us from being the unique people of God.

God intended our sexual drive to draw us to the one person to whom we commit ourselves in marriage. Sexual intercourse should be the expression of love and intimacy between husband and wife. Yet, often, sexual desire becomes selfish and is used as a tool to coerce others. Through sex, people use one another as objects of pleasure. The sinful corruption of sexuality leads to the very opposite of true love. In our day, we are well aware of how deadly sinful sexual desire can be.

There are other desires, natural to us as creatures of God but often perverted by sin. The list includes our desire for attention, accomplishment, pleasure, entertainment, security, convenience, comfort, competence, and knowledge. All of these, though quite natural, can become sinful. Peter says abstain, have nothing to do with any desire or longing that becomes sinful.

How do we know when a desire should be resisted and rejected because it is sinful? Peter answers, "[They make] war against your soul" (v. 11). He's not talking about "soul" in the sense of a hidden, invisible part of you as a person. "Soul" in the Bible refers especially to our relationship with God. Here's the principle: Anything that draws us away from God, rather than closer to God; anything that cools our affection for Jesus, that will not help us become more like Jesus; anything that stands in the way of doing what God wants us to do—anything like that we must avoid.

Note the implication: You and I can know a sinful desire when we see one. Obviously, some of them will be common to all. Among them are a fascination with entertainment promoting sexuality outside God's will, the enticing desire to have more than we do and to be discontent with what we do have, the drive to excel at the expense of others, the urge to repay evil with evil. In addition to these common sinful desires, each of us could probably list others that especially threaten to make us less than the holy people of God. Lest we fear being unaware of threatening sinful desires, the Holy Spirit will surely reveal them to us if we will listen.

Peter also implies that you and I *can* abstain from all sinful desires. However strong they may be, we can steer clear of them. Remember, Jesus has redeemed us (which means "set us free") from these very desires and the way of life they represent. "You know that it was not with perishable things such as silver or gold that you were redeemed from the empty way of life handed down from your forefathers, but with the precious blood of Christ, a lamb without blemish or defect" (1 Peter 1:18-19). Precisely because Jesus set us free, we may and we must "rid [ourselves] of all malice and all deceit, hypocrisy, envy, and slander of every kind" (2:1). Even more bluntly, "[Jesus] himself bore our sins in his body on the tree, so that we might die to sins and live for righteousness; by his wounds you have been healed" (v. 24).

When someone slips away from God, it's never by accident. Nor is there any such thing as a spiritual kidnapping. It's always because choices were made. Desires were embraced and not rejected, and that created distance from God. Peter assures us that this need never happen. We *can* abstain. On the basis of Jesus' death and resurrection, the Spirit empowers us to reject *all* sinful desires.

God not only works directly in our lives, supplying the strength we need, but also works indirectly through the means of grace. These are wonderful gifts from God to His family, designed to nourish us and keep us healthy as His children. Through the Scriptures, prayer, sharing with other believers, worship, and serving others, God strengthens us to reject sinful desires and grow in our relationship with Him.

The fact is we are either walking away from God or toward God. Peter's advice is to move toward God, to come closer, ever closer. Stay away from anything or anyone keeping us from drawing near. As we draw near, we are taking care of our souls, our relationship with God, so that together with our brothers and sisters in the Lord, God forms us into His family.

The second half of the mandate for accomplishing our mission calls us to "live . . . good lives among the pagans" (2:12). He takes it for granted that we will live among, and interact with, unbelievers. Commonly, holiness had been misunderstood as a call to have no contact with unbelieving people, especially if they live in clear or blatant immorality. Indeed, some branches of the Christian church have made a specialty of disassociating from the unsavory elements of society, but clearly that's not the way of Jesus. Ironically, disassociation in the name of holiness may actually be a sign of *unholiness*. Any brand of holy living that keeps us from interaction with those who most need God's love is foreign to the way of Jesus. That means it is not the way of holiness.

To be sure, the Bible everywhere calls God's people to be different from other people. That's the basic meaning of holiness. But we must be different the same way Jesus was because He is the basic model of holiness. While Jesus established close friendship ties and deep fellowship only with His disciples, still He was constantly among the people, interacting with them, regardless of their unsavory character. Actually, from the Gospels, we gather that Jesus devoted major time and energy among the people. He got close enough to know their names and their histories, close enough so that they could form an opinion of Him, and close enough so they wanted to come even closer.

Our mission as holy people requires us to follow our Lord. We must interact with unbelievers enough for them to see who we are, what kind of stuff we're made of, how we react to people and circumstances. Especially when we're under fire, experiencing adversity, mistreated by others, falsely accused, we must be close enough so they will see our responses. When they do, they will be attracted. They will wonder about Jesus. They will be drawn to the God who makes us family and uses us as priests in the world. On the final day, many of them will join us in praising God.

To be like Jesus and to live a holy life requires us to interact with unbelievers so they can see Jesus in us. While that's a challenge each of us must meet individually, part of the church's mission must be to encourage us to meet the challenge. Again, the climate and mood of the church plays an important role here. Our leaders must model interaction with unbelievers. Their example not only shows us how to do it but also sends a powerful message to the Body: this is OK and, in fact, expected of our members.

Having created a climate where such interaction becomes the norm, the church can devise ways to give members "permission" or encouragement to develop their gifts and abilities in order to make an impact on their world. We must help one another to understand that God calls people to be "priestly" custodians, librarians, homemakers, accountants, physicians, nurses, attorneys, teachers, construction workers—you name it. In every field of endeavor, unbelievers need the ministry of the priestly people of God.

In the name of mission, it seems to me, the church must adopt the mind-set and develop the strategies of a missionary task force. Within the family fellowship of the church, members are formed, trained, equipped, confirmed, commissioned, and deployed as missionaries during the week. Church will become not so much a place to which we come as a place from which we go to do our mission as the holy people of God. The church should consider changing its vocabulary, modifying its schedules, and altering its programs to become truly "mission-al" in these ways and others.

What a mission! God calls us—individually and collectively—to penetrate the world as members of His family in such a way that many will take note, see in us something real and authentic, and turn toward God. This mission is blatantly priestly in character. It does not aim, at the outset, at the restructuring of society, the resolution of the great social and moral plagues of our time, or the reformation of human government. In spiritual ways, as we pursue our mission, God will bring transformation in all of these areas. Our lives will model Jesus' way of life, proposing a radical alternative to the world's ways on which current social, political, and cultural reality rests. Then, when unbelieving people turn toward God and join the family, God will have them already in place and will use them to shape their environment in ways that please Him.

Peter gives examples of how this works in the lives of oppressed slaves (1 Peter 2:13-15), of Christian wives facing opposition from unbelieving husbands (3:1-6), and of persecuted house churches facing social harassment (3:8 and following). In each case, Peter expects, and later history demonstrates, that when God's people accomplish their mission, transformation occurs not only within individuals but also within the social, cultural, and political structures of the world.

Notice that both halves of the mandate must be observed in order to accept our mission. Caring for our personal relationship with God, abstaining from all that hinders us, and drawing ever closer to God are essential if we are to live the good lives that will have impact upon the unbelieving world.

Obviously, we must be close enough to unbelieving people so that this impact can indeed occur. Being God's holy people calls for a balance between internal care for our souls and external interaction with unbelievers.

Maintaining that balance challenges us. In most churches, people tend to rally around one or the other half of the mandate as if it were either/or. Either we focus on things we do at church *or* on meeting people's needs in the community. Either we're content to be in the sanctuary *or* to be in the soup kitchen. We may imagine we are free to embrace one and not the other, based on personal preference. So we may care about cultivating our walk with the Lord but not about helping others who do not yet walk with the Lord. We may love to be in the "house of the Lord" but care little for letting our lights shine in the marketplace. Or we may love to be out "doing for Jesus" but have a hard time tolerating worship.

When it becomes either/or, we're just a step away from neither/nor. When it's neither/nor, the church will be *neither* the family God wills *nor* the priesthood He desires.

Let's not forget we're seeking to be like Jesus. He was one with His Father-God, yet constantly interacting with people, drawing them to a new life. Our mission requires nothing more or less.

Mission Impossible

In the TV program, the tape-recorded message outlining the mission always concluded with a summary that began with the words, "Your mission, should you decide to accept it, is . . ." In a sense, there was a choice. Yet everyone knew there was no real choice—not if the director were telling the truth and not if Jim and his cohorts were the sort of people we knew them to be. There was no question they would accept the mission and accomplish it. The only question was what sort of creative and ingenious things would these agents do to accomplish their mission? That's what made each episode so exciting.

It's the same for us as the holy people of God. Our Director tells us the truth, and He calls us to accept a mission of life and death and eternal consequence. We *do* have a choice. Yet, if we are the people God calls us to be, the people we claim to be, the choice is obvious. Nor is there any question about the outcome of the mission. Accomplishment is certain.

Isn't this mission truly impossible, especially for the likes of us, especially for the churches we know? Can we really expect to become a family of brothers and sisters in Christ whose belonging to each other takes priority over every other sort of human belonging? Can we truly envision being such a family—living to welcome others, not waiting for them to come to us but moving out in mission with eagerness to serve people everywhere with priestly devotion? And for these reasons, could we make the world sit up and notice how strange and alien we seem to be? Or are these things truly impossible?

At one critical point, the mission God calls us to accept as His holy people is *not* like an episode of *Mission Impossible*. We do not depend on our ingenuity and creativity. No indeed! In this respect, also, we're called to follow Jesus.

As we've seen, when Jesus began His mission, He cited the words of Isaiah. He said, "The Spirit of the Lord is on me, because he has anointed me to . . ." (Luke 4:18). It was in the power of the Spirit of God that the Son of God accomplished His mission. Similarly, when Jesus conferred the mission upon His followers, He promised them that the Spirit would come upon them and empower them to accomplish their mission. The Book of Acts tells the story, or begins to tell the story. When the Spirit came upon the followers of Jesus on the Day of Pentecost, they proclaimed the mighty deeds of God (2:1-13). By the Spirit's gift, their proclamation drew people from all over the world. Before the day was over, those very people had become a new kind of people, a new family. Immediately, we begin to read about their close, caring fellowship that attracted new folk on a daily basis and made them at home with God. We also read about the awesome work of the Spirit in their family-fellowship that caused them to reach out to others with power, to meet every sort of human need, and to see others join the family. This was a fellowship that could, and did, embrace people of all ethnic and cultural backgrounds—Jews and Greeks—and that could offer daring forgiveness and acceptance even to Saul of Tarsus, a former enemy who was now a brother (9:10-19, 26-30; Galatians 1:18-24). Not perfect, by any means, but still they became a family the likes of which the world had never seen. Truly they were a family of strangers and aliens, seeking the welfare of all people with priestly devotion. They were a holy people on a mission.

Our mission is not impossible because we have access to the same Spirit of God. His power makes the mission Jesus gives us not a mission impossible but a mission accomplished. Let the church wait, pray, and seek the fullness of God's Spirit, and let the world beware!

Background Scripture: Genesis 1:31; Luke 4:18; Acts 2:1-13; 9:10-19, 26-30; Galatians 1:18-24; 1 Peter 1:18-19; 2:1; 2:11-15, 24; 3:1-6, 8

CHAPTER 11

Facing the Reality of Suffering

I DON'T KNOW ABOUT YOU, but I hate "fine print." More often than I care to admit I've signed up for some great deal or responded to an advertisement only to learn that things were not what they seemed. Of course, the "fine print" at the bottom, which even eagles couldn't see without corrective lenses, told the whole story. Here are a couple examples:

- While leafing through the newspaper, my eye catches an ad. It announces "super-saver" fares for flights from coast to coast, a promotional campaign for a new airline company. Unbelievably, it costs only $39 each way from New York to Los Angeles. Then I notice a small asterisk at the end of the line. Below, I find the matching asterisk and with a squint I read, "The following restrictions apply: four-year advance purchase; must travel on a Monday between 3:10 and 3:15 A.M. on odd months of a leap year; subject to availability; prices may change without notice."

- Once I saw an announcement in the paper about a new way to buy used cars—by phone. I had to read it twice to make sure I hadn't misunderstood. Seriously, I was just a phone call away from a new set of wheels. Then at the bottom, in fine print, I read, "When you call, please ask for our sales representative Mr. Hurt." Something inside me whispered, "This name is prophetic. Get involved with this, and it will hurt."

When we "sign on" to follow Jesus, we don't need to worry about "fine print" or hidden messages. Everything is out in the open, written in large print. No one can miss it. According to the New Testament, following Jesus will lead to controversy, conflict, and suffering.

Before we go on, let me clarify something. Followers of Jesus, like all people, often suffer simply because they are human, and they live in a world where bad things happen. This sort of suffering does not discriminate—old and young, male and female, rich and poor, from our culture and from all cultures, believer and unbeliever. All human beings share this common experience of uninvited and unmerited suffering, but that is not our focus in this chapter.

In addition to these common human experiences of pain, there is a form of suffering for followers of Jesus. It is suffering that comes simply because they do, in fact, follow Jesus.

Suffering for Jesus

When I first met Terry, he worked for a local power plant. One of his duties called for the routine inspection of pressure gauges located around the plant. As long as things ran smoothly, these inspections were routine and, well, boring. But if a problem arose, his hourly inspections would prevent disaster.

Terry's coworkers had no use for Christianity or any faith at all. They branded Terry a pious fool and took every opportunity to make his work life miserable. One evening they began to ridicule him, lured him into a shoving match, and delayed the next round of pressure gauge inspections. Wouldn't you know it, that evening a rare problem arose. Had Terry been delayed a minute longer his suffering (along with everyone else's for miles around) would have ended in a huge explosion. Instead, Terry "saved the day," but his supervisors noted the close call. Guess whose work record now carries a blemish for on-the-job negligence? First, he suffered the ridicule and abuse of his fellow workers. Then he, the true victim, is blamed for nearly blowing the place up! All because he took Jesus' call to follow seriously. If Terry would just "go along to get along," the suffering would end, not to mention the benefits to his career. But Terry remains a follower of Jesus.

All around the world today similar or more sinister forms of suffering assault committed followers of Jesus.

Seventeen Christians die each hour somewhere in the world for their faith.[1] An estimated 200 to 250 million Christians are at risk. "We are not talking about mere discrimination, but real persecution—torture, enslavement, rape, imprisonment, forcible separation of children from parents."[2]

I suspect we don't begin to know the depth of suffering that afflicts the followers of Jesus today. Here's the truth—no fine print. Following Jesus has and will always lead to conflict and suffering. Why? Let's turn to Peter's first letter as a primary source for answering the question.

Holiness Means Suffering

As we have seen, followers of Jesus are holy people. At the beginning of his first letter, Peter describes his Christian readers with "holiness" language. They are "God's elect, strangers in the world . . . through *the sanctifying work of the Spirit*" (1:1-2, emphasis added). To "sanctify" means "to make or set apart as holy." The sanctifying work of the Spirit makes people holy. That's why Peter characterizes Christians—followers of Jesus—in this way.

One of the primary commands Peter gives comes early in the letter:

As obedient children, do not conform to the evil desires you had when you lived in ignorance. But just as he who called you is holy, so be holy in all you do; for it is written: "Be holy, because I am holy" *(1:14-16)*.

In the life of all true followers of Jesus, God's Spirit is at work to make them like God. Since that is true, they must embrace what God is doing and refuse to return to their former, ungodly patterns of life. Being holy means being different. Just as God is not like other gods or powers, so His people are not like other people.

What happens to people who are different? A 10-year-old comes home from school, complaining about his clothes. When he left to catch the bus in the morning, he couldn't have cared less about the clothes he was wearing. But *now* he cares. His clothing is not like what the other kids are wearing. So they made fun of him, didn't include him, and made him feel lousy. The other kids made him suffer for being different.

Watch carefully what happens the next time you're in a room crowded with people and someone wheels in a severely handicapped person. Immediately the atmosphere changes. No one looks directly at the disabled person, though everyone looks, stealing quick side-glances when it seems safe to do so. If people were laughing, suddenly they become serious. If people were talking, often they lose their train of thought. Perhaps a child innocently blurts out, "Daddy, what's wrong with her?" Of course, none of this happens intentionally, and most of us would never dream of hurting the disabled person. Yet, almost always, the person in the wheelchair observes these reactions and finds them painful. Because the person is different, he or she suffers.

My wife grew up in southeastern Ohio in the midst of a strong Amish community. In fact, her family was the only "English" (non-Amish) family in their little village. Through the years, she became a friend to many of her Amish neighbors. Sadly, however, these cordial relations could not be taken for granted. Several years ago, an Amish buggy was run off the road by a car, and a little girl lost her life in the accident. Unfortunately such accidents occur too often in that part of the country, despite the frequent caution signs along most roads. In the weeks that followed this particular accident, the investigation uncovered the shocking truth. It wasn't an accident at all. The young people in the car, bored on a Friday night, decided to find some Amish to harass. Because they are different, the Amish suffer.

That's the way it is with followers of Jesus. Since we are holy, which means different from others, and since the world around us *is* hostile to people who are different, we will suffer.

How Following Causes Suffering

We don't look to the world for models and examples of how to live the holy life. Instead we look to and learn from God, as Jesus reveals Him. Let's consider how following God's direction will likely lead to suffering.

Good exposes evil. Because we have been rescued from dead-end living, we should recognize no obligation to walk on dead-end paths. So Peter urges us not to allow our lives to be controlled by sinful human desires (see 1 Peter 1:14; 2:11). We are free to say no to whatever is not good. Likewise, we are free to say yes to the good.

How angry people become when they learn that their way of life is not good, especially when they learn this from us! Not because we make it a point to tell them, but because we live in a way that shows them. Sometimes exposure leads people to embrace the light, but at other times it leads them to snuff out the light. To be like Jesus may lead others to do the same to us.

Joyful suffering may increase hostility. Often when people experience hardship and suffering, they complain and grumble. Even though believers suffer simply because we are different, we don't complain. "In this you greatly rejoice, though now for a little while you may have had to suffer grief in all kinds of trials" (1:6).

When others see that sort of joy, they will do one of two things. Either they will follow Jesus, or they will want to make His followers sorry.

Following Jesus' example in suffering may lead to still more suffering. Peter encouraged his readers who were household slaves to follow Jesus' example when their masters mistreated them.

"To this you were called, because Christ suffered for you,

leaving you an example, that you should follow in his steps. 'He committed no sin, and no deceit was found in his mouth.' When they hurled their insults at him, he did not retaliate; when he suffered, he made no threats. Instead, he entrusted himself to him who judges justly" (2:21-23).

Perhaps we're tempted to think that if we respond to suffering the way Jesus did, things will improve. That does not always happen. As we saw before, responding to suffering as Jesus did will lead our attackers to one of two reactions. Either they will be amazed at us and wonder why we are different, or they will become even angrier.

Followers of Jesus live with an eternal perspective. Peter told his readers that their lives were part of an eternal plan. "And the God of all grace, who called you to his eternal glory in Christ, after you have suffered a little while, will himself restore you and make you strong, firm and steadfast" (5:10).

God has not given us merely a new *lease* on life or even a new *start* in life. He has given us a *new* life, a life of an entirely different order.

[A] new birth into a living hope through the resurrection of Jesus Christ from the dead, and into an inheritance that can never perish, spoil or fade—kept in heaven for you, who through faith are shielded by God's power until the coming of the salvation that is ready to be revealed in the last time (1:3-5).

To follow Jesus in this entirely new kind of life is to live out of the future or to live every day with an eternal perspective. We regularly submit to the "Ten Thousand Year Test." Here's how it works: In evaluating the concerns, causes, and circumstances of life, we ask, "Will this matter 10,000 years from now?" If so, we pay close attention, adjust, and even suffer. If not, it's probably an ultimately trivial pursuit.

While living with eternal perspective will encourage some to receive new life in Jesus, it will enrage others. To be in the world but not of the world, as Jesus was, causes both responses from unbelieving people. That's holiness, and that's why holy people will sometimes suffer.

Holiness and Suffering Today

As I write these words, the persecuted Church in other parts of the world has recently come into the world's spotlight. We should use every opportunity and means available to relieve the sufferings of our persecuted brothers and sisters around the world.

At the risk of misunderstanding, however, I think there is something strange in all of our outrage over the suffering church. What is strange is our shock—as though we are surprised to hear that Christians are suffering for their faith, as though we assumed that the world had moved beyond such hostility to the gospel.

We sometimes sound as if we view suffering for the faith as an exceptional or extraordinary experience. Yet, historically, suffering has been a common life experience for the faithful people of God. Rather than the rule, perhaps our more comfortable brand of Christian life in the West represents the exception to the rule.

This possibility prompts me to consider some hard questions. Why don't we suffer more than we do? Is it simply because our environment is relatively open and friendly toward faith? If that is so, then why have we not made a deeper impact upon our culture for the Kingdom? Or does our relative comfort in following Jesus suggest we have become too friendly and accommodating toward our environment? Does our limited suffering signal a lack of holiness?

Since our culture allows us relative freedom from suffering, compared to others around the world, why don't we see more fruit? Why doesn't the supposed openness toward spiritual things lead the Church to an expanding influence for Christ in our society and to redemptive impact on its ill? Or are we not a threat to the status quo, at least not enough to make anyone really mad?

Hard questions, aren't they? They have sent me back to the Scriptures for a refresher course on what it means to follow Jesus. Even a quick review reminds me that following Him makes us different. In a Jesus-rejecting world, that will lead to situations of conflict and suffering. The Scriptures convince me that our comfortable patterns of Christian living and, even more, our surprise at the suffering of others uncover a need for God's holy work among us. These hard questions also drive me to prayer —to seek the God whose presence makes us holy and who will distinguish us clearly from the social, political, moral, and spiritual chaos around us. I have to believe, when God does this work among us, suffering will have a larger place in our lives.

Yet I am greatly encouraged. I'm convinced that the young people among us are showing us the way. A couple of years ago, several young people decided to follow Jesus through the witness of friends in our youth group. These new Christians came from families who held nominal memberships in mainline denominations. When their sons and daughters started eating, sleeping, walking, and talking "Jesus," they became very "interested" in religion. More specifically, they were interested in saving their kids from going "off the deep end." As a result, parents pressured their kids to renounce the faith, or at least to be "more reasonable." They forbade them to go to our church. They threatened to kick them out of the house. And they bad-mouthed the church as "a sect that is breaking up our family." In other words, both the young converts and the church God used to disciple them suffered. Following Jesus seriously led them to a confrontation with real hostility and threat in their daily lives.

I'm encouraged to think of our young people showing us the way. To be sure, many of them are immature and in need of ongoing nurture and guidance. Yet their devotion to Jesus and their zeal to be all He wants no matter the consequence beckons us all to follow Jesus seriously enough to suffer.

I'm convinced this represents the wave of the future—

more, not less suffering. The radical commitment of these young people, marking them as fanatic disrupters of the status quo and leading them to suffering, is the call to holiness that God issues to the church. If we are to have a future, I believe it must rise out of such commitment. It's the only future God offers us.

Observe again, God doesn't dabble in "fine print." Plainly, following Jesus as the holy people of God means conflict and suffering.

Why would we want to follow Jesus if that's what it means? Don't we have enough heartache and suffering as it is, simply because we are human? Why would we add to it? Three simple answers:

- First, it is Jesus who calls us.
- Second, following Jesus places us in the sweep of an eternal story—from before time to beyond time.
- Third, following Jesus assures our participation in His final victory.

Then, how could we follow Jesus in such radical ways? Especially in the West, our love of comfort and ease, and our skills in acquiring them, make it hard for us even to imagine a life flowing out of such radical commitment, not to mention actually living that way. Again, three simple answers:

- First, Jesus died and rose again to free us from all that would hinder our following Him faithfully and radically.
- Second, Jesus sends the Holy Spirit to put into effect all He promises us.
- Third, Jesus calls us to walk not only with Him but with one another. The community of God's people—the family of God—that we become when we follow Jesus provides a rich and necessary resource for living the holy life.

Following Jesus on the way to holiness means suffering. In response to both the "why" and the "how" questions, I've offered three simple answers—simple but not easy. Remember, there's no "fine print."

Background Scripture: 1 Peter 1:1-6, 14-16; 2:11, 21-23; 5:10

1. Private letter from Dr. Larry Houck, World Missions General Director, Free Methodist Church, August 27, 1997.

2. Nina Shea, "The Global War on Christians," *Reader's Digest,* August 1997, 51.

CHAPTER 12

Thriving in Community

I REMEMBER THE FIRST TIME each of our three little girls walked. What a thrill for them and for us—party time for the whole family!

However, it didn't just happen. None of our girls, nor any other child for that matter, simply walked "out of the blue." There were milestones in their physical development that had to be passed. They had to develop to a particular point. Yet, even with the physical requirements met, learning to walk wasn't mastered entirely on their own. We didn't send them to lectures on the dynamics of pedestrian mobility. Nor did they watch a video. Since they couldn't read, the latest how-to book was no help. Our girls learned to walk in community. These little people saw family members on foot, and it made them curious. They observed that walking is faster than crawling, that walking people are up higher and can see and reach more. Soon they decided they might give it a try.

Family members encourage their little ones to walk. When the first faltering steps lead to a tumble, the family is there to pick them up, brush them off, apply bandages, and cheer them when they try again. Finally, with just a few steps mastered, families make a feature-length film and call Grandma and Grandpa to share the joy.

Children learn to walk within a community of walkers. Without that community, learning would be so much more difficult.

How Do We Learn to Walk?

Little children must find their first steps scary. Likewise, walking like Jesus sounds difficult, even intimidating. We've seen that followers of Jesus trust God no matter what, especially when tough times come. We recognize the things that would ruin our relationship with God and reject them. Similarly, we understand what will enhance our relationship with God. Jesus' followers hang tough and bear up under pressure. Though we suffer insults from others, we love even our enemies and find ways to show them God's goodness.

How do we learn such things? Just as we cannot reasonably expect infants to walk, talk, and relate to others on their own, so we cannot reasonably expect to follow Jesus fully on our own. If we are going to live a holy life, we will need support, encouragement, and help from others. Everyone needs *community.*

The early Christians would never have questioned their need for community. It was a foregone conclusion that all people would be taught and powerfully shaped by the group to which they belonged. In turn, individuals would help shape the others who belonged to their group. In fact, belonging to others was the foundation for personal identity and life.

How strange this sounds to modern ears! Some modern folks insist that the individual, rather than any group, stands at the center of the universe. "Please, I'd rather do it myself," my children sometimes say to me and to others whose help they truly need.

In contrast, the Bible assumes that we live in community and that the community plays a critical role in who we are and how we live, for good or ill. Most of the commands and instructions God gives us in the Bible are in the plural. God addresses us as His people first and only secondarily as individuals. That's not just because the Bible was written to groups; we often speak to groups and make special applications to individual lives. We do this because our culture prizes individualism, and we want to make sure each one understands and applies the truth.

The biblical writers didn't go out of their way to make specific applications to individuals as we do. That was not because individuals weren't important to them, but because individuals were not *all*-important. The community or the Church is the primary target of the Bible's truth, and the writers assumed that they were communicating with all members of the group.

Even more important, the community was and still should be target of the truth, because the truth comes home to individuals most powerfully when heard, received, and lived within the community. According to God's Word, we need each other to help us walk, talk, think, act, and react as the holy people of God. On our own, we are like children who assume they can do everything by themselves. Of course, it just doesn't work that way.

Jesus in Community

Jesus demonstrated our critical need for one another in the family of God. If ever there could be a spiritual Lone Ranger, you'd think the Son of God would qualify. Yet, He sought and cherished community. Jesus' public life and ministry flowed out of the fellowship He established with the 12 disciples. Though Jesus was starting the Church and training His followers for their ministry after He left, He was also modeling the need we all have for community. Because Jesus was human as well as divine, I think He was also satisfying His own need for fellowship.

Jesus did not regard community—the family of God's people—as merely an option. Indeed, community stands at the heart of God's plan for His people. Apart from this fellowship, we simply cannot become who He calls us to be. It is not surprising that the Early Church developed a rich and dynamic fellowship. Jesus told His disciples to await the promised Holy Spirit and they did—together. The Spirit's invasion of their lives was corporate as well as individual. In fact, the most powerful feature of the Early Church's witness seemed to be their fellowship. The community itself proved nearly irresistible in its attraction to unbelievers.

The Body of Christ

The whole New Testament speaks with one voice about the importance of community. God nurtures and matures the life of His people when they are in deep, loving relationships with one another. The most famous New Testament imagery for the church—the human body—makes this point powerfully.

> The body is a unit, though it is made up of many parts; and though all its parts are many, they form one body. So it is with Christ. For we were all baptized by one Spirit into one body—whether Jews or Greeks, slave or free—and we were all given the one Spirit to drink. . . . If one part suffers, every part suffers with it; if one part is honored, every part rejoices with it (1 Corinthians 12:12-13, 26).

Just as it is impossible to have live body parts without a living body, so it is impossible for individual followers of Jesus to thrive in isolation from other followers. How grotesque it would be to see an eyeball rolling around at will, with no connection to a head or body. Or to observe a hand or leg detached from arm or hip! Each of us needs the Body—the community or family of God—to be alive and well as the holy people of God. Within the fellowship, we see clearly who we are and how we may do God's will. Likewise, within the fellowship we grow and become like Jesus. The Scriptures offer no hint that any of this can happen apart from community, but they do promise that, within the community, God's Spirit will empower His people to follow Jesus consistently and convincingly in the world.

God Creates the Community We Need

Holiness thrives within community, but not just *any* community. Not just any gathering of warm bodies will do! Often a church community or fellowship turns out to be a collaboration of like-minded people. Or if not like-*minded*, alike in some other way—ethnically, socially, economically. What binds them together are their similarities.

Yet being in a group of people just like we are may, in fact, only encourage individualism. Suppose I gather some people who think and act the way I do. Then when we're together, we discover we share many of the same tastes and preferences (surprise, surprise!). We're so comfortable and feel blessed because we're so at home with one another. Of course, others are welcome to join us, but we notice that only people like us seem interested. Of the interested, just a few ever actually join our group. What I've just described is what many a church has become—a group of folk bound together by their similarities. Belonging to such a group reinforces those characteristic similarities and encourages us to be satisfied just the way we are. Nevertheless, underneath the similarities may hide all manner of things that never see the light of day because they are our unique problems, hang-ups, and growing edges.

In a community bound together by similarity, it isn't safe to be different or unique. When differences surface, the group usually offers two options: resolve the differences so that we once again fit together or leave. A community formed primarily on the basis of similarity tends to reinforce its members' self-centeredness and individualism. This kind of community will not tolerate the deep sharing that helps us become like Jesus.

We cannot simply decide to form a community whose members learn how to walk like Jesus. God alone can create the community we need. Our natural families help us understand this point. We don't decide who our families will be. Nobody asked me if I preferred to have only brothers and no sisters in my family of origin. I had nothing to do with the makeup of the family. Others composed the family and then put me in it. Likewise, a couple does not decide what sort of baby they will have (at least not yet!). Their family comes into being as a creative, surprising miracle.

That's the way it works with the spiritual community or family we need as the people of God. God *creates* the community independent of human wisdom or power. Once we are born into the family of God, we find ourselves members of a community He has created.

Actually, God designs the Church of Jesus Christ as an odd assortment of people. Within the community He creates, there are people who would probably never get together on their own. Consider some examples from the Scriptures.

On the Day of Pentecost, the Holy Spirit invaded the lives of Jesus' first followers and made them a large church—in excess of 3,000 people. From the beginning, the Church created by the Spirit included all sorts of people. We know that in the Pentecost congregation were people from most parts of the known world (see Acts 2:8-11). While most of them eventually returned to native soil, they still experienced a fellowship in the Spirit unlike any other fellowship they had known. In time, the movement of the Spirit crossed every cultural and social barrier and created family, even among those who had been bitter enemies. The community of God's people could not be explained in sociological or demographic terms. God was creating a community that would help His people learn to walk as Jesus walked.

Paul concludes his letter to the Romans by greeting a number of acquaintances. The names may strike us as strange, but studying the names of Paul's friends and the things he says about them reveals what a miracle God performs in creating community. (See Romans 16:3-16.) Scholars tell us that these names suggest a group including male and female, slave and free, wealthy and poor, professional and laborer, urban and rural. This community has people of every social and economic stripe. Even more astounding, Paul describes this wide range of people with family terms, using words like "mother," "brother," and "relative." Then he says these people relate to one another in ways ordinarily reserved only for family members. They risk their necks for each other (v. 4). Or they greet one another with a holy kiss, affection much too intimate for non-family (v. 16). In other words, in the community God creates, we find people we'd never expect to be together in a family.

This still happens today. We have seen it, if indeed we have experienced the Church as a community created by God.

When I was in graduate school, my program of study put me together with six other persons—a United States Presbyterian female, a Latin American Presbyterian male, a Lutheran, a Canadian Mennonite, a Free Methodist, and a Roman Catholic. I cannot imagine any other set of circumstances that would have brought all of us together, but over time, our association became a fellowship. Our common commitments to Jesus and the Scriptures drew us together. That fellowship, I'm convinced, was a creation of God, for only He could have given us the sense of family we enjoyed in those years and from which each of us greatly benefited.

In the summer of 1993, my wife and I went on a short-term mission to South Africa. Over a five-week period, we found ourselves, members of a white minority, warmly embraced by our brothers and sisters in South Africa. Time and again, despite the differences between us, we experienced a harmony of spirit and depth of sharing that surprised but delighted us. The community God created among us challenged us and led us to change.

One of these changes for me involved my preconceived notions about worship. It's hard to be rhythmically impaired among happy, dancing Africans at worship. Before I left their fellowship, even I was moving to the cadence of the African worship songs. My awkward attempts were not simply an effort to fit in but expressed a freedom of worship I'd never known before. Though my performance was certainly laughable, I believe the Father smiled, much the way I smiled at the sight of my babies' first wobbly steps.

We don't have to go somewhere exotic to recognize the miraculous character of the community God creates. In most congregations we can see how God has brought together an unusual assortment of people. I've had the privilege of pastoring churches where the wealthy and the impoverished sit in the same pew Sunday after Sunday. Where young people actually listen to and like old people. Where farmers and professors have coffee together because they enjoy each other's company. Where businesswomen and homemakers bear one another's burdens. Where Republicans and Democrats work as partners in ministry, to name only a few of the common connections.

How do we explain these connections that make community? I know only one answer: God is at work creating a new people—His family. That He uses the most unlikely combinations as witnesses to God's power.

It also witnesses to God's plan. In the community He creates among us, we demonstrate God's will for all people. The barriers that separate us from God and from other people collapse. The fear that makes people suspicious and hateful has been cast out. And the selfishness that corrupts relationships of all people has been overcome. For in this kind of community, we who were made in God's image actually begin to look and live like Jesus.

Spiritually speaking, we learn to "walk."

Background Scripture: Acts 2:8-11; Romans 16:3-16; 1 Corinthians 12:12-13, 26

CHAPTER 13

God-Created Community

HOW DOES GOD CREATE the community we need? To answer this question is a bit like answering, "Where do babies come from?" Even though we have a scientific explanation, when it's all said and done, there remains an element of mystery. When a baby takes the first gasp of air and cries, most observers of the birth feel they've witnessed a miracle. The community that God creates and we need qualifies for miracle status as well. How do we explain a miracle?

Perhaps the best place to begin is simply to acknowledge God's creativity. In the beginning, He created the universe out of nothing. That fact should settle once for all the question whether God can create the community we need, for when He created the first human beings, He made them for each other. God's statement, "It is not good for the man to be alone. I will make a helper suitable for him" (Genesis 2:18), was not just a reference to marriage. God was affirming the communal nature of all human beings. In the very beginning, we were made to be our "brother's keeper" under the loving lordship of our God. When sin disrupted everything, including our ability to relate to one another, God's saving plan envisioned total restoration or re-creation, including the community so important to our well-being.

God's creative and saving love works both *vertically* between God and us and *horizontally* between others and us. Community, therefore, is part and parcel of God's plan of salvation for all people. And the whole plan of salvation works through Jesus by the power of the Holy Spirit.

As I reflect on this, I realize that we are often guilty of sharing only half the Good News. We boldly proclaim Christ's death on the Cross as God's great reconciling work. We say, "No matter how bad you've been and no matter how you've treated God in the past, Jesus' death will make peace with God. Accept the gospel and enjoy a loving relationship with God as a gift."

But that's only half the good news. Shouldn't we also declare that Christ's death on the Cross tears down walls of hatred and bitterness that divide us from others? On the basis of God's Word, shouldn't we expect that Jesus would mend our broken relationships with others as much as we expect Him to mend our relationship with God? I think so.

The Importance of Love

Again we must ask, how will this happen among *us?* How does God work with each of us so that together we become a community? I'm convinced that we're more than halfway there when we realize that God creates community through Jesus by the power of the Holy Spirit, and this is a miracle.

The miracle of community begins in our individual hearts. God must first give us the capacity, that is, empower us for the *love* that leads to community. Peter describes it this way: "You have purified yourselves by obeying the truth *so that* you have sincere love for your brothers" (1 Peter 1:22, emphasis added). Notice the words "so that." They tell us that "obeying the truth" purifies us, which results in a sincere love for others. Peter clarifies in the next verses: "For you have been born again, not of perishable seed, but of imperishable, through the living and enduring Word of God . . . the word that was preached to you" (1:23-25).

On our own, we cannot love as we need to form the community God desires. Though we were made to reflect God's likeness and love, sin has taught us to look after No. 1.

By nature, we become individualists—either proud of our independence and personal achievements or bitter and broken over our failures and needs (probably a mixture of both). Apart from God's help, we cannot reach out to God or others as we were made to do. Someone must save us from ourselves and our selfish preoccupations. Someone must give us a new life capable of deep love for God and others. Of course, Someone has—Jesus rescues us from our self-centeredness.

Paul put it like this, "God has poured out His love into our hearts by the Holy Spirit, whom he has given us" (Romans 5:5). We become people able to reflect God's likeness and love. The community we need comes within reach through Jesus' work and by the power of the Holy Spirit.

God then expects us to use the capacity for love He's given us. The fact is that we can have the ability to not use it or stop using it. Just because we *can* love doesn't mean we *will*. At the root of every broken relationship and community lies a failure to love.

Indeed, the command to love is the supreme command Jesus gave His followers. "I give you a new commandment, that you love one another. Just as I have loved you, you also should love one another. By this everyone will know that you are my disciples, if you have love for one another" (John 13:34-35, NRSV).

The command to love has both a positive and negative expression. If we love, we will do certain things. Likewise, if we love, we will not do certain other things. In general, we will not do, think, or say anything contrary to love. Yet, we can be even more specific, because the Bible is.

Peter, for example, expresses a positive command. Since the truth has cleansed us of selfishness so that we *may* love, "love one another deeply, from the heart" (1 Peter 1:22). The language Peter uses carries great intensity. He's really urging his readers to become a community of "intensive care." What does that mean?

He answers by expressing a negative command or prohibition. Have nothing to do with unloving attitudes and words among us. I like how one modern version puts it: "Stop being hateful!" (1 Peter 2:1, CEV). That we have the capacity to love as Jesus did doesn't mean we are no longer able to hate and become bitter. These destructive emotions can get hold of us. We must recognize the danger of this when we experience disappointment in others, as we certainly will, and allow no place for hatred or bitterness.

Peter continues, "Quit trying to fool people, and start being sincere. Don't be jealous or say cruel things about others" (2:1, CEV). We've all felt tempted to be someone other than we are, to pretend rather than be real. We also sometimes compare ourselves with others in the community. As a result, we feel as though we are better than those less fortunate and inferior to those more fortunate. This leads to pride or jealousy. Often the tongue becomes the weapon of choice to cut people down to size. Still, none of this can keep company with love. God's Word says to get rid of every trace of such things.

Because we have the capacity to love, we can be free of these negative attitudes and avoid acting and speaking contrary to love. That's a tall order, indeed, but this is God's work through Jesus by the power of the Holy Spirit. His mighty work forms the basis for our consistently loving relationships with one another.

Perhaps that's the way it should work, but what happens when we fail to love? What happens when we give in to temptation and say or do something unloving? Even then, the capacity for love can show us the way. Over and over the New Testament stresses forgiveness, bearing with one another, and admonishing one another. There is good reason for this emphasis. In any human community there will be failure. Still, in the community God creates, no failure is beyond recovery.

Peter expresses this beautifully when he says, "Love each other deeply, because love covers over a multitude of sins" (1 Peter 4:8). Don't misunderstand, love doesn't condone or excuse sin. Instead, love creates community where we understand what it means to be human—to make mistakes, to fail. It's a community where it's OK to be human but not OK to be unforgiving. Love creates a community where forgiveness may be sought and received. Again, that doesn't lead to indulgence but to accountability, owning up to wrong, restoration to fellowship, and transformation. Love forgives and makes people new.

Will We Live in Community?

We need the community that only God can and does create. It's more simple than we might think, though not easy. The full gospel proclaims a radical and comprehensive reconciliation—both with God and with others. Jesus died and rose again, and His finished work provides the foundation for community. No barrier to the sharing we need with others can stand in the face of what Jesus has already accomplished. My kids would say, "It's a done deal!"

God's Holy Spirit creates community on the foundation of Jesus' work. Wherever people welcome the good news—committing themselves to Jesus as Savior and Lord—and are open to the Spirit's indwelling presence, community cannot help but happen. And what a community! It made the earliest believers so faithful to Jesus that not even martyrdom could shake them. It led them to care for each other's needs in ways that amazed the unbelieving world (see Acts 2:43-47). It supported them when they faced harassment and persecution from the authorities (see, for example, 4:23-31; 12:1-17). And it provided the powerful and positive peer pressure necessary for them to live out the gospel in radical ways. Apart from such community, these early believers could not have survived as the holy people of God, much less thrive.

This community that God creates and we need is not a relic of the past. God's Spirit continues to activate the finished work of Jesus among people, creating community. For example, astonishing reports come out of China these days, estimating a network of faithful Christians numbering in the millions. Certainly one of the keys to this miraculous growth of the church is the close-knit fellowship of the house-churches. Despite unbelievable pressure and persecution from the government, God has used this fellowship to produce Christians who are a threat to worldly powers. This happened in the 20th century, but it sounds like 1st-century Christianity.

I recall my own first days in love with Jesus. The sharing and caring of comrades in faith was absolutely essential. Without their support, encouragement, and occasional rebuke, I'm not sure where I'd be today. Since those first days in faith, the most intense spiritual growth has always come through deep sharing and caring with the community God gave me. As a pastor, I hardly ever see people who are growing, becoming more and more like Jesus, and using their gifts for God and others apart from vital connection with others.

Presently, one of my greatest joys as a pastor comes from watching the young adults in my church—senior high and college students, even some middle-schoolers. In chapter 11, I told you about several young people who came to know Jesus and suffered the misunderstanding of their parents and worse. It's fair to say that they were won to Jesus in the first place by God's power at work in the fellowship of our young people. Then, when these new believers faced pressures to stop following Jesus, their new brothers and sisters held on to them. Literally, the power of love within their community kept them from renouncing Christ. Even more, those tough times weathered with the help of the community actually strengthened them in the process. When the pressure let up, they were more committed to Christ's way than ever. Because the community held on to them in love, they gained a firmer grasp on the Lord. Again, it happened in the 20th century, but it sounds like the 1st century to me!

I yearn for the whole church to know this same essential community. Without it, the holy life and its deepest joys simply cannot be lived and known. I remind you, the work is done—Jesus has laid the foundation and the Spirit of God wants to make it real for us. If we have begun to walk with Jesus, you and I have the capacity to love. The only question is what we will do with the command. *Will we love?*

I want to ask two questions to urge you toward application of the truth. First, *is there anything that keeps you from loving as Jesus loved?* Ask the question sincerely and prayerfully. It's a question God will not leave unanswered. If He points out anything, let His Spirit cleanse the barrier away. Let Him give you full capacity to love.

Second, *are you in community with others right now?* I'm not asking only if you go to church or if you are faithful in devotional or service activities. Rather, are there some folk with whom you share deeply and regularly—who know you, who support you in living like Jesus, who can ask you the tough questions, people for whom you can do the same? God's Word assures us that without such people, we will never find our proper stride on the way of holiness. His Word also assures us that He will provide the community we need. It is His will.

God is at work to create the community we need, and in my heart's eye, I see God raising up a new generation of Christians:

- People overwhelmed by how God shows himself in Jesus, barely able to believe how deeply God loves them and unable to help but love Him in return.
- People whose sense of God's undeserved forgiveness prompts a reflex response back to God and to others who deserve God's love no more than they do and to whom it is no less offered.
- People who, therefore, hunger and thirst for more of God and whose appetite God satisfies.
- People who find themselves by losing themselves in Jesus, who find themselves now oriented to God, others, and self the way Jesus was.
- People whose dependence on God leads them to value and depend on the family God gives them in Jesus, who discover how deeply they need this family to con-

tinue following Jesus—even when it means costly sacrifice, service, and suffering in order to do what Jesus
would do.

- People who know *they* could never be or do as God
  calls them, and yet they *are* and they *do,* because God
  empowers them by His Spirit.
- People whose former brokenness is clearly on the
  mend, whose relationships reveal a beauty and attrac-
  tiveness that many of the love-starved and sin-stained
  folk around them will find irresistible.

It seems right to think that among such people as these,
consumer-oriented Christians stand a good chance of seeing
how trivial their pursuits are when compared to following Jesus. Some of them may grow passionate about being all God
calls them to be and begin having the time of their lives.

It also seems right to think that among such holy people,
the broken, addicted, and deceived of our world will see the
true way of life with its promise of healing, freedom, and
peace. No doubt, some of them will become brand-new persons!

Of course, reality falls short of what my heart can envision. Yet it falls short only because God and the world still
wait for a people to hear God's call and receive God's empow-
ering to be like Jesus. God and the world wait for people like
us to show our love.

Background Scripture: Genesis 2:18; John 13:34-35; Acts 2:43-47;
4:23-31; 12:1-17; Romans 5:5; 1 Peter 1:22-25; 2:1; 4:8